RUDE

KATIE HOPKINS
RUDE

Biteback Publishing

First published in Great Britain in 2017 by
Biteback Publishing Ltd
Westminster Tower
3 Albert Embankment
London SE1 7SP
Copyright © Katie Hopkins 2017

ISBN 978-1-78590-246-8

10 9 8 7 6 5 4 3 2 1

A CIP catalogue record for this book is available from the British Library.

Set in Minion Pro

Printed and bound in Great Britain by
CPI Group (UK) Ltd, Croydon CR0 4YY

MIX
Paper from
responsible sources
FSC® C020471

CONTENTS

I AM NOT A TWAT

Well, not a complete twat, anyway.

I appreciate many people think I am about as big a twat as it gets. Yuge, as The Donald would say. A *tremendous* twat. Some would go as far as to say they can't stand me, and even talk about hate – as in, 'I hate that bloody woman' – which seems a bit extreme.

Liberals say we must Hope not Hate, but maybe this only applies to people who think the same things they think, because liberals tend to hate me more than most.

And I get it. I really do. I have lots of opinions on lots of things that feel very personal to many people. The way they look, the way they feel and how they should handle everything from kids to depression. I have views on the choices people make, like how to spend cash and how to vote. And even on arbitrary stuff, like the way people navigate Argos stores and stand open-mouthed as their goods descend from the heavens on a mad, 1970s-style conveyor belt.

It's all up for grabs in my world. And unlike most people, who say things in the privacy of their homes to their mum or their mates, or on Facebook to their friends, I say things out loud to a few million people at a time.

This month, in one week alone, 45 million people read or shared my tweets.

This was not my design or plan. It just kind of happened. There was a space in the media market for a woman who spoke like a bloke but understood the mysteries of women. And I filled it. And then got paid to keep filling it.

I'd argue that if I were a complete twat, no one would employ me. How could anyone ever work with me if I really was such an utter arse 100 per cent of the time? It would be horrible – I'd be rude to the team and cruel to the makeup ladies. (Then again, I look at the meteoric rise of James Corden, the biggest cockwomble of the lot, and I see that supreme twattishness is not a barrier to success.)

I prefer to address the twat issue head-on.

When I am booked for a piece of work – a talk or a presentation, or the process of getting this book into your bag (for which I am eternally grateful to you, by the way) – I schedule the 'I-am-not-a-twat' meeting. This is how my diary looks:

I am not a twat: BBC Radio Festival.

I am not a twat: talk radio.

I am not a twat: political conference.

I am not a twat: BBC Three documentary.

I do other stuff in between these meetings, in case you were wondering. I don't spend my entire day schlepping to appointments proving I am not an utter spunk trumpet. That would be an exercise in futility.

But it is a useful by-product of the casual face-to-face in

which people who might have to work alongside me get to see if they can.

I-am-not-a-twat meetings are a way of getting people to see the real me. A person I call me-me.

Once you've spent ten years or so as a monster in people's minds, their expectations are pretty low. Most prepare to be insulted, I think. They expect me to come in, spit at the waiter, kick a fat kid, tell someone looking vaguely depressed to damn well pull themselves together, and punch a woman wearing leggings in the face for being so lazy.

And I will admit, most of these thoughts do go through my head. (No woman should ever wear leggings as an outfit choice. They are the devil's clothes and look universally crap on everyone apart from Elle Macpherson.)

What people actually get is this strange little woman with a big nose and newly bleached blonde hair. 'A shit Ellen De-Generes' seems to be the most common description. Or 'an over-excitable puppy dog', according to the *Evening Standard*.

I was once booked to be a speaker at the Annual Radio Festival hosted by the BBC. It's a fairly prestigious kind of event – big names get invited to speak, and important people attend. Sensible types, stalwarts of the airways and random big names like Dermot O'Leary are booked to entertain or bemuse an audience of left-wing media types who look like they are sucking lemons in the rain at a funeral they didn't want to attend.

Being the BBC equivalent of Ebola, I was only invited to talk thanks to the perfect storm of having my own radio show on LBC, the lady in charge knowing a bit about me from working with Jeremy Vine, and the theme: 'disruption'. From a BBC perspective, apparently, I am as disruptive as a heavy period at a swimming gala.

I booked my 'I-am-not-a-twat meeting' with the brilliant woman who runs the event, whom I came to love for being hugely enthusiastic about everything. Sure enough, ten minutes in she said, 'You know, you're nothing like I expected.'

This is a pretty standard reaction to me. And what it really means is, 'Holy hell, you aren't the utter twat I thought you were.'

It's a funny thing: when everyone thinks you are a complete twat, there is only one way their opinions can go. And that is up.

I could probably turn up at meetings and be a bit of a twat and get away with it. Maybe wipe my cutlery with antibacterial wipes. Or tell a crying kid to do one. Because when the starting bar is so low that President Erdoğan would be considered highly tolerant, the world is your oyster.

I want this book to be a kind of handbook for life. Much of it will be about the things I have completely stuffed up, and I hope that by sharing my tremendous failings, I can prevent others from repeating my mistakes.

So I feel obliged to say to any young people reading this that the whole 'I-am-not-a-twat' lark is not a course of action I want you to follow. I am not suggesting for one moment you spend your life earning a reputation so maleficent that when people actually meet you they are pleasantly surprised.

This is an insane and hugely inefficient strategy, sort of like letting your child poop on the pavement then having to go around and pick it all up before you can start your day. No one needs that in their lives. You can ensure you are not perceived as the biggest bastard in Britain, or the biggest bitch in Britain and cut out the middle man.

Not that I am suggesting you should make it your aim in life to be nice. Christ on a bike, that's just offensive. Funny, sparky, rude, fabulous, queen – yes. Nice – no.

My class three teacher, Sister Bede, used to say, 'Never use the word nice,' and I think she had a point. Who wants to be nice? It is one of the least exciting words in the English language. We've got clunge. Frisson. Bamboozled. Dearth. Bombastic. Rank. And the best some people can manage is 'nice'?

To be completely fair, Sister Bede was anything but nice herself. As with most religious individuals, she was reason enough to run from Jesus as fast as you could and keep on going.

Sister Bede had multiple other issues in addition to her intolerance of the word nice. A life of celibacy wearing only navy blue, with an unsightly head covering, and dodgy beige shoes had made her deeply bitter. She probably endured chronic chafing from excessive vaginal dryness as well. I can only imagine the flaking into those 30 denier tan tights with reinforced gusset.

She made it her special calling to make my life hell.

She used to make me stay in over lunch break and write lines with my right hand to 'improve' me. Even though I was left-handed. I am pretty certain if she had been a Catholic priest, things would have taken a more sinister turn.

I'm guessing she did it all in the name of Jesus, or some such piffle. But I say to all nuns (and priests): just because you do it in the name of Jesus doesn't make it right.

If I stabbed a kitten through the eyeball in the name of Jesus, the RSPCA would still prosecute me for kitten cruelty. And rightly so.

Despite accepting her advice to avoid the word nice, you could argue that if half the country already thinks you are an arsehole, you have taken things a bit too far. You can imagine what it's like when I rock up to give a talk somewhere, in front of a few hundred people. The twat thing happens there too. People book me to give talks about my life, the economy, capitalism, the state of the nation – all sorts of stuff. One of my favourite talks is: 'We are not all equal, some people are just not worth the effort'. It is best performed at universities and other places where leftie liberalism is so pronounced that kids virtually have to murder a Jew on their way into the lecture theatre to prove their anti-Semitic credentials.

(Unless you have a Hezbollah flag waving out your arse and an almost psychopathic aversion to Israeli mangoes, you can no longer get into the Russell Group universities I used to aspire to as a child.)

I am an odd booking as a speaker. Typically it goes like this:

Excitable Hopkins fan in position of administrative power is told to book a speaker, and books me.

Many other shy Hopkins supporters are secretly excited and there is a change to a bigger venue to hold the numbers now anticipated.

Some Hopkins haters get wind of the event and, failing to consider the option of JUST NOT TURNING UP, decide to get outraged instead.

A fat woman from HR decides that outrage is her territory

and wades in. It's payback time for every outspoken thing I have ever said about chubsters, and the fact I call fat people lazy. And because I can wear a size 8 trouser and she can't. And she has bad highlights.

A panellist or other minority individual says they will pull out if I am allowed to speak or am given a platform.

The big boss has to make a call. Big audience, big publicity and the potential that I am not a twat versus keeping the chubsters and women with issues happy.

Sadly, many choose the latter, which is never the right decision.

But when I do manage to get past the HR/chubster mafia, my audiences and I have a lovely time together.

For many, this is genuinely the first time someone has stood in front of them and told them to say and ask whatever they like without thought or filter, and to be as blunt as they like.

It's pretty darned therapeutic.

At Harrow, in front of 800 young men – future leaders of our country all congregated in the Churchill debating room – I asked the assembled throng: 'Hands up if you think I am a complete cow.'

It usually takes a few brave or sparky souls to kick them off. But once the feeling of a confessional takes hold, it spreads faster than syphilis on a Saturday night in Scunthorpe.

Soon most of the room was there with their hands up, laughing. It's a glorious thing in so many ways, being honest about someone to their face – and a rarity in modern times.

Only a few stalwart Hopkins-lovers remained, arms at their sides. I love them for their loyalty. And perhaps because they had already peeked behind the monster mask and seen a regular woman who actually finds herself pretty funny.

I admire the boys at Harrow hugely. They have been gifted the best education money can buy. Undoubtedly most of them know riches most of us can't even imagine. They have multiple homes, London apartments at sixteen, and accept it as standard that they have access to the best of anything they might want.

But the pay-off is that here they work damn hard. Prep: 7 a.m.–8 a.m. A full day of school. Supervised prep: 6 p.m.–8 p.m. And 800 of them still turned out, in full uniform, for a non-compulsory talk at 9 p.m. I am overwhelmed by the dedication of these young people to learning. It makes my heart thud with hope for the future.

Sometimes after these talks – which are pretty noisy by virtue of the fact that it's me versus the room – some of them come up and are genuinely cross: 'I came because I hate you. And I expected to go on hating you. And now I am confused.'

And I suppose that's the thing in life. If you are perceived as being an utter bellend and turn out not to be, it is a bit confusing. A bit like finding out your kindly parish priest is a paedophile, or the local WI is actually a brothel for the over-sixties, but in reverse.

I reckon if you disagree with the things someone says, it is easier just to hate them. Better, almost. If they are a monster and you hate them, you can dismiss everything they say as monstrous and consign them to a box marked 'evil'.

If it subsequently turns out the monster is actually pretty likeable, funny even, and one of your mates wants a selfie with 'it', what does that mean for their horrendous views?

There is always a pivotal moment when my audiences realise 'someone actually quite nice thinks these terrible things'. And it makes them question what they thought they knew. What if other nice people think this stuff?

Which is why some people at my talks are positively cross that I am quite nice.

They cannot compute the fact that an actual human with a heart is able to sit on a sofa with a 24-stone woman and say to her face that they would not employ her because she is too fat. Or look someone in the eye and tell them they are slow. Or inform full-time mums that they are actually unemployed.

We just aren't used to anyone being that direct, especially not a woman.

I am no raging feminist with a desire to scrawl graffiti on my tiny tits, but I do think if I were a fat man with a regional accent I would be doing stand-up. Unfortunately, posh-sounding white women are not funny, and that's a fact. Even common-sounding fat ones can barely raise a smile. See Sarah Millican for details.

This is what has given me a platform and a voice: being a woman. With an opinion. Who never expected fans so doesn't try to please them.

I've learned to accept that some people will not always like what I say or do, and that they now have the tools to be able to tell me so (though rarely to my face). Sadly, many lack the vocabulary to articulate what they actually want to say, so they are reduced to name-calling, mocking the size of my nose, or offering to rape me with a machete instead.

Put people in cars and they act in exactly the same way. In

the heat of the moment, with little time to think, they shout, swear, flip the bird or slam their hand onto the horn.

Twitter is like road rage. And it should not be taken personally.

Or reported. I honestly believe Twitter needs to police itself. It should not be draining resources from actual police, who sometimes seem to spend more time dealing with hate crime online than crime on the streets.

The Mayor of London, Sadiq Khan, set up a new £1.7 million hate-crime hub, staffed by a team of five, just to police Twitter. Particularly my Twitter. After any terrorist attack, it goes into overdrive, logging hate crimes and assisting the police with messaging against Islamophobia.

It is a mad world where burglaries go unattended but Twitter results in arrests.

Back in the glory days of Twitter, before you could complain about threats of violence and Twitter was obliged to look as if it gave a toss, I grew used to the violence expressed online. Hardened to it, I think.

When people said they were going to set my car on fire with my kids in it, I knew they didn't mean it, and weren't really going to come and do that.

What they meant was: 'Stop saying Tyler is a terrible name.' Stop laughing at the fact that my Destiny has her fucking future all mapped out. Or my Bella is actually shit ugly.

If your son or daughter has those names, my criticisms sound personal. So I can see why people feel the need to be personal back. It makes sense.

I have had the same six or so friends for twenty years. There are new additions, of course, and plenty of notable others.

But my main fall-back of family and friends have all lived through much bigger-ticket items than my being a bit well known. Or notorious.

My girlies have stood by me when I've made far bigger mistakes than the odd ill-worded tweet. My first marriage, for example. They all knew it wouldn't last. But they all turned up to the wedding and were kind and agreed to be there for me if it all went spectacularly to hell in a handcart – which it did, and they were.

Once people suss out I am less of a cow than they actually thought I was, they feel the need to rationalise it somehow. We are programmed to want an explanation for everything. And trying to explain away the twat/nice-person gulf is no different.

The 'twat/nice-person' gulf is not a phenomenon unique to me. When you think about it, it occurs in other areas of life as well.

When you meet your ex-husband's new girlfriend, for example. You will have decided in advance that you hate her, and rightfully so. No one ever likes their ex-husband's new girlfriend. Particularly if she is the reason you are no longer married.

But it can turn out that she is actually rather nice. And then you will have to make the journey across the twat/nice-person gulf.

My parents regularly cross this gulf. They are not racists, but they were born in a time and have lived in a place where you aren't local unless you live in the same house your grand-father grew up in and have inherited the beef cattle farm. 'He's foreign, but he's actually rather good,' is a direct quote from my mother about her new optician, who comes all the way from remote Essex. Foreign, but good. This is the foreign/actually-quite-capable gulf.

These are popular explanations for the inexplicable notion that I might not be a complete arsehole:

'I used to hate the old you' – as if somehow it was me that changed, not their opinion.

'I suppose you have to be tough to withstand all the hate' – as if I am to blame for making myself into a monster, casu-ally forgetting they were the ones doing the hating until ten minutes ago.

'If you're married you can't be all that bad' – as if my hus-band was a character witness in a murder investigation.

'Maybe you were edited to look like a cow.'

This kind thought follows the logic that all the good bits of me being nice and human were left on the edit-room floor, and all that was used was spliced footage of me being an utter git to the people I was sharing a space with.

Rule number one of TV land: never blame the edit.

Only complete narcissists blame the edit. People deter-mined that the watching public shall see them as saccharine sweet, or at least vaguely intelligent, at all times. Which, frankly, isn't true of 95 per cent of the population.

One third of the British public has an IQ below 85. That's the sort of intelligence where you need to be introduced to your own reflection in a mirror. Or taught how to use Velcro.

Or where to put a toothbrush, even though the clue is in the name.

The edit suite can only edit what you have said. It can't put words into your mouth. And the media will tell it as they find it or as their audience will believe it to be true.

If you agree to be filmed for something, you sign off on the whole package – not just the carefully crafted side of you your agent would prefer people to see.

I tend to think that if you don't like what is being said about you, you should get your face out of the media and get on with your life.

When people ask how I handle all the grief I get online, I tell them it was my decision. I signed up for *The Apprentice*. I pursued a career in the media, and if I don't like it I can sod off back home and sit on my sofa.

It's a truly modern curiosity that famous types only too happy to earn a £2 million advertising contract with L'Oréal because they are a 'well-known face' choose to take legal action against the media when they feel their privacy has been violated, or when a story emerges that has not been curated for public consumption.

Gary Lineker is a perfect case in point, happy to coin it in as Walkers' biggest crisp salesman and to gob off about migrants and other subjects that fit his liberal agenda.

But one teeny-weeny story in *The Sun* alleging a few tax naughties and the lawyers descend.

These celebs are dodgy estate agents of their own lives, happy to display the well-maintained exterior that looks good in pictures, and hiding the structure that reveals their house was built next to Chernobyl and is suffering from chronic damp and subsidence.

Of course we all do that to some extent. What is makeup if not a concealer of the cracks in our face we prefer not to show to our work mates? But celebrities take this camouflage to ridiculous extremes.

No one trusts estate agents and you shouldn't trust famous faces either. Unless you are buying hair dye, and then it's probably OK.

Being able to understand that if you put yourself out there, not everyone will like what they see is fundamental to survival. Personally I think it should be taught in schools.

It's the same message I gave to my friend's daughter when she cried because someone called her fat when she posed in her new dress: if you don't like what people might call you, don't pose in a tiny dress on social media. When you are eleven.

How stupid do you have to be?

Despite all the cotton wool we wrap our kids up in these days – no one is a loser, everyone gets an A* just for showing up, and the school counsellor is as important as your maths teacher – we have singularly failed to teach them that not everyone will like everything they do. Some people will hate it. And if you don't want to hear the bad stuff, don't revel in the good stuff.

Don't be a naff celebrity. Don't enjoy making five figures out of a shampoo and then complain when your privacy is invaded on holiday. These things are symbiotic. Suck it up.

In November 2017, I completed the first Stand Strong School Tour to try to embed some resilience into our young people – it was a programme specifically designed to help kids form their own opinions and deal with the tough stuff in life.

It is important kids are given space to think, to talk a lot and to shout out if they are bullied or afraid. But we singularly fail to teach them how to deal with the turbulence of life – the person who ignores you, or calls you fat online, or gangs up with a group on social media to humiliate you or cut you out.

How to handle being rejected from the chat group or the party list. How to sit alone and feel happy with yourself. How to take a barrage of criticism and find the lines you'll think of later and wish you had been quick enough or brave enough to say at the time.

I school my children in these things on a daily basis. They tell me their worries, or what some nasty piece of work has said. And I suggest the response I would have given.

And that is usually: embrace it. Embrace the hate and anger. Imagine swallowing it like hot chocolate. Then breathe, and respond with something that puts you on higher ground.

Make like a processing factory for insults. You take them in, you absorb them without being contaminated by them, and you recycle them triumphantly as power to your own elbow.

I imagine myself as a swimmer diving into a pool. Hands above my head. Pointed toward the water. And then diving into the criticism, watching it slip past my sides. I keep moving forwards. And I leave them all behind.

Or an arrow whistling through the air, wind at my sides. Just about catching the odd word of the shouty people all being cross as I streak past.

It's all a game of power. You have it. You hold on to it. And don't let them take it from you.

I think the game goes on in our daily lives all the time, especially if you're a woman.

A friend who notices you've lost weight might say, 'Strange, we always seem to lose it from the places we don't want.' Or no one comments on your new hairstyle. Or your news.

Or perhaps you think you look pretty good that day but no one comments on your dress. Or perhaps someone says something snarky instead of something kind.

A whole world of rejection and small slights which can add up to making a rubbish day feel super-rubbish.

You are in control of all of this. You do look good. Your hair does look nice. It is fantastic that your son or daughter has done well and you are proud of them.

You do you.

My mother and I have a saying which is now employed extensively throughout my private network (outside of work): 'Be positive or piss off.'

My mother also used to say: 'If you haven't got anything positive to say, say nothing at all.' I clearly didn't heed that advice too much as a kid. And frankly, when my father was asking 'what happened to the other 5 per cent' when I scored 95 per cent in my exams, neither did he.

So, inside my little bubble of family and friends, I have taken it up a notch. 'Be positive or piss off' is not about avoiding honesty. If someone needs some honesty in their life, they will get it.

But day to day, on the periphery of things that don't matter all that much but might make someone feel stronger or better about themselves, I am right there.

If I feel you are hurting, I will be right there by your side. It doesn't matter if you have loved me, hated me or even voted against publishing my book. Your happiness still matters more to me than this book, or words on a page, or what people might say. Let them talk.

Shaming is something that is done to you. Reject it. Refuse to be shamed. Yes, I had sex in a field. It felt great. Are you jealous?

I urge it in others. Own you. If you look good, feel good. If you feel a bit rubbish, tell someone and ask them to help make you feel better.

And if someone wants to put you down, or chip away at you or steal some of your happiness – ask them not to.

Yes, I have lost weight. And no, I don't mind where it comes off. I feel great.

Yes, I am proud of my son. He has worked really hard for everything he has achieved.

If you find yourself in a scorpion's nest of sisters more toxic than a forgotten Tampax, earn points by seeing how many of them fail to comment on how brilliant you look. Or how nice it is that you have your home, or your family, or your pyjamas to look forward to later.

The queen scorpion might be your boss, but you are the Queen of Sass – and that's frankly all that matters.

This is my kind of feminism. Making strong women feel more self-assured. I think this is the kind of feminism we need in schools as well.

Less time spent looking outwards for social slights, or calling out perceived inequality, or fighting to be heard, or reporting sexism on portals such as Everyday Feminism – which is essentially a cave where mad women shout with each other to no collective purpose.

And more time building inner resolve, a core of resilience – like muscle – helping you to stand strong in the face of it all, despite the fact your boiler has just broken down, one of your kids has just been excluded or you've put on two stone and feel like a fat, frumpy fool.

Yes, my nose is big. Well done for spotting that.

Yes, I do look like a horse. Paddy Power Racing sponsored by university degree.

A shit Ellen DeGeneres? I was hoping for hot lesbian book-seller. But I guess I will have to make do.

My family all hate me? Fair play. But I buy their Christmas presents so that is going to be disappointing for them.

You wouldn't have sex with me if someone paid you? I am not certain that is how prostitution works. But you would know better than me.

Accept. Swallow. And take the power from their wrath. Make like an arrow and keep moving forwards.

Smile, breathe in and out, and watch your breath rise up. Now follow it.

Even better, stick your shoulders back, put your head up and remember that the people who love you matter the most. They probably think you are fantastic. Go you.

CHAPTER 2

THE POWER OF THE FOOF

Vagina.

It's a small word. But super powerful. More so if you drop it in to a conversation unexpectedly, with a side order of straight face and direct gaze.

For some unknown reason, most of my serious conversations about my life or career take place with middle-aged white men who feel the need to tell me off for something. Or tell me I can't do something. Or tell me 'it is more serious than we thought'.

This applies to everything from my medical issues to my Twitter feed.

Sometimes it's the police, telling me off for a tweet. Sometimes its compliance, telling the radio station we have yet another Ofcom complaint about something I said on the radio.

The best way to handle any of these serious situations is to use the word vagina. Just drop it in there when no one is expecting it, like a surprise dog poo in the recycling bin.

It tends to clear the room pretty quickly and make important people scrabble to get away from the bad smell.

My boss once tried to tell me off for using the word pussy live on air. (I was actually talking about the feminist marches in America after the inauguration of Donald Trump – the 'pussy marches'.) Pussy is on the secret list of words you aren't allowed to say because they are offensive; he argued it was the same as saying fuck live on air.

Clearly it isn't. And to imagine I would sit on live radio on a Sunday morning at ten o'clock and say 'fuck' is preposterous.

Most of my audience were good men and women of Britain, happily preparing their roast dinner in their kitchen while listening to me. We chatted along together and I was ever-conscious that children might be listening.

I also went on to say that the pussy marchers' banners were ridiculous; one strident lesbian was wielding a placard that informed the crowd 'My pussy is made of steel'.

On air, I went off on a rant which included the line: 'Yours is made of steel? Well, I can fit a can of coke in mine – sideways.'

People complained about that, too. (In its original iteration it was a 24-ounce can of Coors; I was writing a column for the *Daily Mail* and had one on my desk. So I think I deserve credit for being culturally astute and making the switch to something more European.)

I was called in to have a formal and serious conversation with my boss. He read and re-read the phrase 'I can fit a can of coke in my vagina – sideways' from the Ofcom transcript of my show. And wanted to know if it was a joke.

Can you imagine trying to keep a straight face, in a serious meeting with a small, deadly pale and sincere white man who used to work at *The Guardian*?

Every bit of naughty me was shaking with the effort of looking concerned. Even my boss's minder (or his deputy, as he preferred to be known), another thin white man, lost it and laughed.

I told him I had intended to be funny; I have never tried to fit a can of Coors or Diet Coke in my vagina sideways. But that there was possibly an element of truth to the statement given my second baby weighed twelve pounds.

I saw his pitiful member visibly shrink at the thought.

Men are hopeless in this situation. The word vagina is like daylight to a vampire. They shrink, go puce, imagine potential sexual harassment charges and get the hell out of the room as quickly as their little legs will carry them.

It works with women too. Especially ones at the BBC with deep voices and ugly clothes who take themselves way too seriously.

I was once asked onto the very serious *The Media Show* by the very sensible presenter who clearly wanted to prove herself by taking on The Hopkins. Despite inviting me to speak to them (for the benefit of their ratings), the producer told me they wouldn't be paying for my travel because they are the BBC. At which point I replied, as I always reply in such cases, that I would be back in touch when I had registered for charitable status.

It always amazes me how people sat on a big fat salary and pension plan, funded by my taxes and yours, are so quick to point out I will not be paid for the contribution they have invited me to make.

Or when I am invited to talk and then told 'we are a not for profit, so we don't pay a fee' as if I don't understand the basic accounting principle that profit is calculated after salaries and their wages are taken out. You don't work for free. Nor do I. None of us can feed our children with hot air. Though lefties do try...

Travel expenses secured, I dutifully went on their terribly serious show in the damn awful mess that is Old Broadcasting House.

And during our conversation about libel on Twitter, in which she was hoping to make me look as thick as the tabloid whore she believed me to be, we got to talking about the defamation law as it currently stands.

I summoned the power of the foof.

'The defamation bar is now lower than my labia,' I declared, watching her brain try to catch up with her face, which framed in a silent scream: 'She just said labia on the BBC!'

In these quiet moments, with your opponent on the ropes, you have time to regroup and work out your next move. Meanwhile, their whole self is preoccupied with the need to not look anywhere near your crotch.

If you ever get the opportunity to discuss your labia on the BBC or any other public platform, I thoroughly recommend it. Owning being female is way more empowering than shouting angrily about mushroom penis men.

I think my labia are genuinely very low. My girlfriends say I clap as I walk. I don't hear it, but I do sometimes wonder if I should dress to the left or the right. The whole conversation came about when we were looking at the before and after photos for *My Fat Story*, where I chucked on a whole pile of weight and lost it again to prove that if you eat too much and you don't move enough, you get fat. Nearly four stone on and four stone off; three months on, three months off.

The before pictures were taken in my kitchen, which was awkward. You can still see them online if you feel inclined – me standing there in ugly underwear while people took pictures of me naked next to my oven gloves and fridge.

I went out and bought grim underwear in skin colour because I don't own any nice underwear, and I'd realised that if I bought nice underwear I would look a bit like a crap hooker or, worse still, Instagramish in a look-at-me-I-think-I'm-fabulous way.

Whereas I know I look like a thin house brick on two cocktail sticks. Which I prefer to keep covered.

Two things happened. People pointed out I am really moley. Which it turns out I am, I just wasn't self-conscious about it before. One irritating git even sent me pics where he had played dot-to-dot with the moles on my tummy and made farm animals and mapped constellations.

Meanwhile my girlfriends became fixated with my foof flaps, which they said hang well below the normal. They have led me to believe their labia are perky-looking bunny ears forming a pert gate for their husbands to open when they're in the mood.

Mine, they tell me, are like the ears of a bloodhound, threatening to engulf any poor sod who happens to chance his pecker near my bat cave.

I'm not sure I would make a very good lesbian. The poor girl would get suffocated by my labia if she tried anything too frisky.

People point out to me that I can have surgery for this sort of thing. When I say people, I don't mean passers-by in the street. People don't literally hear my labia clapping in the street and stop me to offer advice.

I mean my girlfriends who see me naked. Which, I will happily admit, probably happens more often than it should.

But having surgery on my labia is never going to happen. I have too much hoovering and ironing to do to be buggering about with unnecessary surgery.

When you think about it, being celibate would be a massive time-saving in itself.

I have had quite enough of hospitals and surgery and tend to think that if you're going to go through pain, it might as well have real purpose.

I went and had a vein burned off the front of my shin before I had my brain surgery. An ugly vein which I was self-conscious about. The doctor shoved a hot wire up the inside of my vein at ankle height and fed it all the way up my leg to the top of my thigh. And then burned the thing. As he shoved the wire up the vein, every two or three inches he plunged in needles with local anaesthetic to numb the pain.

I think I am quite tough but honestly, it was agony, and something I am deeply ashamed about now. Why put yourself though all that just because you have a knobbly vein on your leg? How pathetic was I?

The vein has pretty much returned as it was before and I am rather pleased with it for making a stand. I think it serves as a reminder that vanity gets you precisely nowhere.

Anyone who has ever had a stent fitted will understand my

point about surgery. When I was very unwell after my brain surgery, I had a PICC line for antibiotics to go straight to my heart. Cancer dudes have them too, to save having a line stuck in every time.

Having a permanent line in is a brilliant thing, and I happen to think it is a great pity humans have not evolved with a little capped pipe for this purpose. Like a petrol tank on a car. It would make medics' and paramedics' lives a whole lot easier, too; the secret truth is that many of them dread trying to get a line in because they are a bit shit at it and lack practice.

The weird thing about doctors is if they need to get a line into your heart, let's say, they always start at the most obscure place. Do they start at your chest? Do they hell.

'We need to put a line in your heart. So we are going to start here, at your left gonad.'

'Ahhh, we need to put a line in your neck. We will start here, in your ankle bone.'

I am convinced it's a staffroom game for medics: see how far away from the target you can start and get a wire through a patient.

The line for my heart started in the inside of my upper arm. That bit that really hurts if you pinch it; see my point? It stayed in for three months, for daily antibiotic doses, secured by three little fish hooks underneath the skin to hold it in place. And it cured me of my festering meningitis, which was a result.

Less of a result was when the nurse in charge of removing it didn't realise mine was the fish hook version, and tried yanking it out from my heart with one almighty pull … maybe she wasn't a Hopkins fan?

After serious surgery, an operation for vanity purposes fails to appeal. Labioplasty is a good example. Gemma Collins tells me she has had hers done. We were in Cannes together for an event organised by Mail Online.

I was hosting a panel with the Fat Jew (christened as such by his good self, not by me, if you were wondering; even I am not that offensive), the Kardashians' best mate, the Cocktail Club founder and a few other randoms. One was a singer from a band that once came somewhere on *The X Factor* and looked petrified.

Not one to waste an opportunity, that night Gems managed to snag the founder of the Cocktail Club. When I came down to breakfast, she was staggering off to bed looking like someone had taken a leaf blower to her hair and a window squeezie to her face.

She gave me the scoop, adding as a parting gift that Mr Cocktail Club had been eating out of her designer vagina all night.

It nearly put me off my ham and eggs.

But vaginas are powerful things. Whether it's stuff going up, in or out of them, they crack on, like resilient little furry friends.

Mine's seen more action than Mosul, without the white helmets. It has been a warzone. And handled unspeakable things.

Three babies have bundled out of there, with me attached to the gas and air bottle like my life depended on it. My lazy middle baby decided to fester in my womb way longer than she should, guzzling food and sugar all the while, and turned into a monster baby. I had to turn on the amateur dramatics to get myself induced, which is all very un-American.

Americans give you your induce date on the same day you have your pregnancy confirmed; it is organised and efficient.

British midwives are a bit like Catholic nuns circa 1960 who consider any interference in the natural order of things to be deeply sinful. They like 'nature to take its course' even if you are clearly going into the summer term when your baby should have been born in spring and your foof is silently weeping at the thought of the watermelon-sized thing it has to pass.

By the time my second daughter squeezed her Arnie Schwarzenegger shoulders out of my pelvis, Poppy weighed close to a stone and looked like an inflatable baby.

People did that weird face when they saw her – like they had chronic wind or were trying not to yawn. That face that is ready to look at something pretty, but sees something ugly instead, and doesn't want to give the game away.

Although, strangely enough, I have never needed stitches with any of them. Never ripped or been cut to get the baby out. I am not sure whether to be proud of that fact or moderately embarrassed. I wonder sometimes if one day I will go to sit on a bar stool and the whole thing will just disappear up inside me, leaving me with three extra legs. I mean, what's to stop it?

It's a bit like those documentaries you see on telly of men who go exploring in underground caves. They wiggle their way through a fairly narrow passage, then all of a sudden they find this massive underground cavern with its own ecosystem and water supply and creatures hanging from the roof and a crazy echo. That's how I see my foof.

I mentioned this recently during a feminist debate at Politicon – a political conference in California. Even pussy marchers went a bit pale.

There have been incidents.

I once tried to have a coil fitted, thinking it would be a good way of not having another twelve-pound baby and avoiding the fact that I am rubbish at remembering to take pills.

Except coils are not designed for fast people. Coils are designed for single mums who aren't planning to have another kid until the council gives them a bigger flat and they find a bloke sure to sod off, and in the interim all they plan to do is watch Jeremy Kyle or go to toddler groups or mope around Primark pushing a stroller and drinking coffee.

If you are a fast and zippy person who considers basic human functions like peeing and periods a complete waste of valuable time, coils are a nightmare.

They have a little wire which dangles down inside your vagina, fairly near the top, for the day someone needs to get up there and retrieve the thing. Like a rope on a loft ladder. Or the dangly cord on your bathroom light.

A thread just like any other thread halfway up your vagina. Do you see where this is going?

And if, like me, you aren't shy about getting up there with your hands to whip in or whip out a Lil-let, it is easy to muddle the two.

And sure enough, I did.

One speedy day I muddled up the strings up my foof, both dangling there like ropes in an indoor gymnasium. With one big tug I dragged my jagged coil half out of my foof. The grippy teeth of the thing embedded themselves into the walls of my vagina like a cheese grater inside a sausage, and I had to walk to my surgery like John Wayne with a hard-on and confess.

You know how people stand way too close to you at the reception desk of the doctor's surgery? And the way the receptionist looks down her nose at you and asks with some disdain why you have dared to come to the surgery? (Like they are actually anyone you want to tell your private medical stuff to – what qualification do they have apart from being bloody rude?)

So the frumpy woman behind me, the scaffolder behind her *and* the receptionist got the full gory details: 'My jagged metal coil is lodged halfway up my vag.'

That shut her up. And the frumpy woman behind me gagged on her own tongue. Only the scaffolder looked vaguely man enough for the news. I imagine that on his truck parked outside there might have been suitable equipment for the task at hand.

Even the nurse couldn't understand it. Too many old people moaning about feeling a bit poorly had desensitised her to the trauma of being an active woman with multiple kids, jobs and commitments.

Showing your foof at the doctor's surgery is a strange thing.

We all dread going to the nurse for a smear test. Any woman who says otherwise is lying. Most of us try to put them off. All of us get nervous and overcompensate by talking too much. For some it is such a humiliation that they simply never go.

I worry about all sorts of things. I want to look trim and

neat, so I get the razor out and try to tidy the bush into something that looks like it's seen a gardener this side of Easter. And I get the scissors at it to make sure there are no long bits which might get caught up in proceedings.

But I don't want to look like I made too much of an effort. I don't want to look like I was out to impress the nurse or make a move on her.

And I don't want to look like my husband and I are still at the Russian hooker stage of our relationship, when the reality is that if I take off my pyjama top I am going all out and it is probably Christmas or his birthday.

And at no point do I want to remove the softening effect of some hair from labia that positively drag on the floor. Consider it like a fringe on an ugly forehead.

The key to retaining some semblance of dignity is a long or at least flappy skirt. This way you can lie on the bed, heels up to your bum cheeks and knees spread to the east and west, without looking like a slapper who is used to having her bum blowing in the breeze.

I can still remember turning up in jeans once, thinking it was an appointment for something else. And being given the equivalent of half a kitchen roll to hide my modesty.

Naked from the waist down, vag out, with nowhere to hide save for fourteen bits of Lidl-quality kitchen roll. A woman's life can be hard.

But also brilliant.

I love that our bits can do all this stuff. Can handle having babies, not having babies, taking smear tests, oozing strange stuff, bleeding more or less on demand – and yet it's still the place straight boys want to put their bits into more than any other place in the world.

What a funny thing it is.

We are born separately. Live as individuals. Are spread about this planet at random and by chance. And yet, as we wander about, we manage to find people who want to poke their man bits into us. When you think about it, it's the weirdest thing.

Brits are notoriously shy, polite, private people. Sharing a lift is agony and most would rather boil their head in a bucket than make small talk on the Tube.

But despite ourselves, we still end up naked. With strangers. Who poke things in places we don't advertise.

Brilliant!

I say brilliant. But with two girls at twelve I'm not always quite so sure. When I think about the things I got up to at fourteen with my first boyfriend, Matthew – well, I don't even want to think of my little babies in that way.

Even as someone with no filter, for whom no subject is off limits, I don't want to think about my own daughters getting up to the stuff I used to get up to. It's a jump too far. I like being the mother of eight- to twelve-year-olds. I do not want to be a mother of sexually active people that want to tell me about it.

My girlfriend said she was trapped at her car steering wheel the other day while her son talked to her about blowjobs and how to ask his girlfriend to do more of what he wanted. And whether that would mean they were in a relationship or not.

There she was. Trapped. Trying to style it out as a cool

mum capable of chatting about blowjobs with her teenage son. She dropped him off and had to go to Costa for a double macchiato, then home for a lie-down.

I don't intend to style it out at all. I've told them I want to know nothing about it. About anything they are up to.

Unless they are in trouble. Any stranger could come to my house and ask my kids, 'What do you do if you have a problem?'

'Tell Mum.'

'What will she do?'

'Sort it out.'

I would bet my house on these replies. I have made them repeat them since they were tiny, in the hope that one day, in their darkest hour, even if they can't remember their own name, where they are or where they live, they will still know they should ask Mum for help.

They know the only thing I will not forgive them for is not asking for my help.

I have spent a fair part of my life reassuring my parents. Telling them everything is good. Telling them I am fine. Often when it is the very opposite of the truth, when I really couldn't be worse – like when the microbiologist at the neurology hospital where I had my brain surgery (who was morbidly fascinated by my case) told my husband, Lovely Mark, she had never seen anyone make it from an infection this severe and that he should prepare to go home alone.

It's an odd thought that at one time in my life, people had planned for me to be dead. Although that's also true on social media, where people plan for me to be dead every other day.

With my own parents, I try to share successes. And hide the failures.

I think I learned it from them. I was always the kid that did well. Came first in class, got straight As, passed Grade 8 violin at fourteen – with distinction – and finished off my piano grades that same year, too.

So when it came to me having a failing, no one wanted to talk about it.

When my epilepsy announced itself with petit mal seizures that absented me from the room for a few seconds, I was nineteen years old and no one wanted to discuss it. I had no one to tell.

My parents couldn't call it by its name. They called them my 'funny turns' and put them away in a drawer so no one would see. These were too strange, not part of the perfect plan, so they were put away in the drawer and dismissed, instead of being sorted.

And so I carried on. With seizures. Hiding them all my life so no one would see the weakness, no one would know the failing.

Seizures which eventually moved into sleep seizures, scaring the hell out of everyone else who didn't know.

I regret this. I regret all this.

Hiding my illness. Hiding my epilepsy. Pretending I was OK because that was my story. Straight As. Grade 8s. Captain of the netball team. Sponsored through university. The kid who won stuff. Getting into Sandhurst. Getting a Regular Commission. Getting a place in the Intelligence Corps. All good. All talked about.

All the while hiding a massive dark truth, believing somehow if no one talked about it, it would go away.

I was left to deal alone with my funny turns. To pretend them away. To keep reassuring everyone who noticed I was having a fit that I was just 'miles away – ignore me, I'm fine!', with a laugh and a shrug. Just keep on running, keep on running. I followed Dora's advice in *Finding Nemo*, 'just keep swimming, just keep swimming', but lost just the same.

I should have got proper help. I should have got it sorted. I should have maybe stopped a while and got medication to help, got a proper diagnosis. I should have told someone that I needed help, I should never have just pretended I could overcome and tough it out to make it better.

I should have got it sorted before I went to Sandhurst. Instead, I was thrown out for my epilepsy when I should have gone to my regiment to serve my thirty-five years.

I do wonder.

I understand you can't have an epileptic with an AK-47. But I cannot understand why I grew up thinking my epilepsy was a flaw, best not talked about and kept hidden away.

My biggest fear is that my kids would have a fit. And my greatest happiness is that I didn't give it to them.

I think this is why I have told my children to come to me if they have a problem and sworn to them I will sort it, no matter what. And if I can't sort it, I will help them come up with the best fix we can.

It's also helped me see that being a parent is not about bragging what your child has achieved or won. What they are good at or do well. You can try your best with all of that stuff, but the real gift a parent can give is to help their children see that health is the most important thing. And how being born without too many things wrong with you is amazingly lucky.

I see it with my son. Mr Perfect Pants. Born easily into the world, not a thing out of place. Arms and legs that work. A brain that functions like other people's. And a pretty little face, the white-blond hair girls dream of, and long lashes like a llama.

We underestimate how lucky that is.

My first daughter has a gene deletion – HNF1B, to be precise.

(Another medical madness; you can tell it was named by male doctors. Probably the same type of men who decide the nomenclature of phone handsets and gadgets like the X300 Delta. No one normal thinks like that. No one normal comes up with random nonsense letters and numbers instead of a proper name. Like lame-arsed marketers tasked with calling a car something female friendly and coming up with the Isuzu P'up or something equally naff.)

Either way, my daughter Wind (Indy-Wind) sees the world at 90 degrees. Which I think is a glorious thing.

She has an incredible memory and is the family storage facility for information. If I am given a number or an appointment to remember, I give it to Indy, and she logs it for later. She is essentially a human Siri. But way smarter.

She doesn't feel fear or nerves. She has a limited sense of pain, so does not fear it. She sees medical encounters as the transactional events they are, not the emotional dramas the rest of us make them into.

She can watch her own blood tests being taken because it makes sense that to get blood you need to have a needle in your arm.

She is flying though her music exams, because as creative as music is, it is based on rules and order. Beats in a bar, notes on a line, discipline.

She is exceptional at hearing bad or difficult news, as she side-steps the emotional fallout and moves straight to what that means, what to do about it, and how that will impact on the next thing coming up.

Logic. Order. Process. Rules. She loves them all.

Kids like her often go undetected in life. Because they are always 'such a good girl' and 'no trouble'. Because they live by rules and understand rules, there's simply no question of breaking them.

Children like Indy-Wind end up babysitting the mentalist, the nutter, the biter and the kid with zero parenting, because they are no trouble so maybe they'll be a good influence on the demon child Tyler.

It's Wind who led to my well-known rant on *This Morning* about kids' names. I said you can tell by the name what sort of kid you can expect.

And the classic examples I gave were picked straight from kids I knew – although for legal reasons I have to make these massive generalisations from any school in the country.

The truth is that this clip went viral because we all connected to a bit of truth in it. Whether we say it or not, we think it, to some degree.

And even if you didn't think it, we all have a name. If we

have kids, we give them a name. And all parents know, when they choose the name, that the child will be judged by it.

It works at the posh end of the scale, too. Walk round the BBC and you can't move for Hugos and Benjamins. The BBC takes its interns from the posh-kid pool, those who grew up in the privileged bits of London.

For a long time after that *This Morning* moment, people would ask me to rate their name. They would come up to me and say, my name is x, is that good or bad? Like I was the arbiter of names.

People also call me out on the fact that I said I hate it when kids are named after places, when, quite clearly, India is a place.

They have a point. And I will let them score it all day. It's a fair cop in a literal sense.

In my defence – and in the spirit of truth – it's just because I am a bit more sophisticated than my critics and have an acute affinity for the Mountbatten/Hicks family and the incredibly fabulous India Hicks.

India Hicks is granddaughter of Earl Mountbatten of Burma, the last Viceroy of India, who was brutally murdered by the bastard IRA. My daughter is my silent two fingers up at terrorists. And Poppy, my second daughter, is named in memory of all British soldiers who died fighting in foreign fields. Fighting for freedom is everything to me, and hopefully will be for my daughters too.

On a lighter note, I love meeting people with names like Wendy, Roy, Claire and Nigel. I always wonder what the mum was thinking when she saw her little baby, all cute and fluffy, in the maternity ward for the first time. I wonder what went through her head for her to look into the bassinet and decide, 'You look like a Nigel.'

I mean, who names a cute little thing Nigel?

Then again, being in a maternity unit is enough to make anyone confused. I hate everything to do with midwives. I hate how bossy they are; I hate the bloody awful red books they use to write down the measurements of you and your baby; I hate all their rules and their nosiness. And I hate the way they talk to you about birthing plans involving back rubs and breathing, or the odd dip in an exciting-sounding birthing pool and don't tell you the reality of what's in store.

It's the equivalent of telling someone they're going to have a tooth out, then bashing their whole face in with a sledge hammer. While some nutter in the background rubs your back and says breathe in. Breathe out. Breathe in.

I only ever went to one antenatal session. On my own. And I hated it so much I never went back.

Who has time to waste indulging themselves in being pregnant, thinking about pain management and drawing up a plan? I laugh when good students trot out to the pharmacist and dutifully buy a TENS machine – a useless tool designed to help with the pain of contractions. It's about as effective as putting a plaster on your stump when you've just had your leg blown off with Semtex.

I blame midwives and the Great Birthing Lie for half the C sections and 90 per cent of epidurals that are hugely over-used these days.

If you can't work out that giving birth is going to be the worst pain you've ever been in, then you are pretty thick.

Although if you have had a bad dislocation of a shoulder or a hip, you've had a reasonable indication.

If you think it won't hurt when something the size of a watermelon with shoulders comes out of the place most women are too frightened to poke a Tampax into without the aid of a cardboard launcher – then you are a bigger nut than you look in those bloody awful maternity jeans.

And if you let some woman convince you that you'll get through it more easily if you sit in a paddling pool making dolphin noises, then you have way too much faith in uniforms and people called Pam. (All health visitors are called Pam.)

I had to stop my Pam from coming to my house. At the point my dear little daughter was starving to death because I sucked at breastfeeding, she told me to get up every two hours to try to feed...

The mammary militia are psychopaths. Breast may well rhyme with best, but paedo rhymes with Speedo and that doesn't make either of those two things OK.

I don't care how you feed your baby as long as it makes you both happy. The idea there is some kind of judgement on you for choosing powdered milk verges on Sharia-level stupidity.

Poor India was so damn hungry by the time I worked out I could squeeze milk out of my boob and syringe it into her mouth, she had lost four pounds. Bear in mind, when she first popped out she only weighed six pounds.

As soon as I got a bottle sorted, she drank for England, burped a few times and slept like a little log.

My daughter knows breast is not best. Happy is way better.

As for Poppy, she didn't escape the curse of her mother

either. She was born without a decent hip socket. None of us knew until the point when she was supposed to walk and instead dragged her little leg behind her like a dead dog on a lead.

The treatment was brutal. I empathise with any other mums out there who have gone through this with their child.

The solution is to break and rebuild the hip. Then put the child in a full body cast, from the armpits down to each knee, with a metal bar cast between the two to keep the hip joint at the angle the doctors want.

Another freak of medical science. If you sat down and asked any mum what would be the cruellest thing you could do to a little child just learning to walk, breaking their hip and plastering them from armpits to ankles would be right up there.

And then, for extra jokes, add a metal bar across the knees to turn your baby into a kitchen-chair shape. Impossible to pick up, carry, cuddle or put down.

For a final flourish, ask your baby what colour plaster she wants on the way to surgery – blue or pink?

Be warned, we are not talking pastels. The pink is luminous, Day-Glo fluorescent. You end up walking about with a glowing, luminescent baby encased in a kitchen chair with a metal bar between the knees.

And your child stinks. There is no kind way to put this. The thing about having a plaster cast from your armpits to your ankles when you're two years old is, of course, that you don't know when you want a wee yet because you're still toilet training.

And even if you did know when you wanted a wee, you

wouldn't be able to go because some smug doctor bloke trying to be helpful has made you into a human kitchen chair.

Essentially, they cut a hole around your bits and hope for the best. Meanwhile the plaster starts to soak up old wee and get damp...

It honks. I mean really honks.

A mother loves her baby when it smells all clean and soft. Like talcum powder. Or baby bath.

Not being able to cuddle your baby is bad enough. Not being able to cuddle your baby who smells like a dodgy nursing home is way worse. We stank. And we stank big time.

And yet my daughter remembers this whole episode as a glorious time in her life. She remembers me camping out in the ward with her on the pull-out chair, the TV in her bed. She remembers the little boy two beds down who cried all night after they operated on his bits and bobs. And the special skateboard her grandad made her so she could propel herself about on her tummy with her arms.

I am proud of her for all of this. For seeing it as an adventure. And for being brilliant and brave.

Now, by some miracle, she has turned into a county swimmer at eleven, and I watch her differently to the way other parents watch their kids. I watch her with wonder. Because I still see the little baby dragging her leg down the hallway, excited by life.

And I still blame myself. For Wind's gene deletion and Poppy's hip. I think my epilepsy pills were to blame.

I cut them back to the point where my fits were about as bad as I could handle, but I still believe I was the one who caused my children pain. And I will always own their pain and feel dreadful about it.

I don't have an answer for that. I only have guilt and honesty. The girls know I think their problems might be my fault.

I wonder if perhaps the only thing you can do if you have made something go wrong is be there while it's put right as best as it can be. To sleep beside Poppy's bed on the ward for a few months. To help cut away the plaster that made her little bits sore. To help Wind make sense of an emotional world that seems impossible to navigate or understand.

Poppy is the real reason I left *The Apprentice*. I needed to be home for my daughter's operation and recovery. If you ended up winning that spectacle, you were supposed to go and live in Brentwood for six months before the final, allegedly working for Lord Sugar.

I wasn't going to be living in Brentwood. Partly because it is a shit-hole. But mostly because I needed to be on the ward with Poppy and to try to give her the chance to walk.

This got twisted by the media into 'childcare issues'. I didn't have childcare issues. I had an injured child to care for and I had priorities: her.

It's a funny thing being a mum. A side of me most people don't see. When I am whizzing about in London, people ask me if I have kids. And I am always thrilled to say I have three.

Not because I need to talk about them or brag about what they have done, but because they are my happiest, most special thing. They are the best thing about me and the best thing I have done.

I love them. And I will never leave them. It doesn't matter if my husbands come or go, if they are born with one father and I need to find them a better one, or if my microbiologist says I am not going to make it, or I am offered a job I can't refuse. I will always be there for my babies. Like any other mum.

Despite what some feminists may try to tell you, true feminists know better.

Being a woman is not about being weak or being a victim. It is about showing you are strong. It's about failing and owning it. And about accepting all of what you are. It is the power of the foof. And you should wield it well.

LESSONS I HAVE LEARNED:

1. Do not underestimate the power of the foof. I encourage all women to use it wisely. In contract negotiations, pay discussions and end-of-year reviews, remember: you are wielding the foof of power. One mention of the word vagina or labia and that smug-looking white bloke pretending to be your boss will dissolve into a mess on the floor. You have the power. Know your value, and ask for what you want.

2. Doctors are weird. Unless you really need an operation, say to make a bit of your body work that doesn't, I'm not sure surgery is worth it. I feel foolish for having my vein removed. It was damn painful. I nearly fainted. All to achieve a leg I don't care if anyone looks at anyway.

3. Midwives are mental. If you are thinking of having a baby, know that it hurts like hell. It's up there with a double shoulder dislocation and is as bad as a car crash. Except you get a baby at the end. Accept that now and prepare to take as much pain relief as you can get, up to the point

where you still know your own name and can feel your legs; you need to be able to push this thing out, not have it ripped from you like a nasty plaster.

Ignore all midwives' advice. And your mother-in-law's for that matter. Do what you think is best or ask the girl-friend who has stuffed up a bit in life and isn't perfect.

Breast isn't best. You being happy is way better. Don't compete at being a mother. Monkeys and cows have babies. It is not a huge achievement, it is nature. There are no awards.

4. Share the failures, not the successes. Having learned to hide my own failures – of which I regarded epilepsy as one – I would far rather my children cracked on with the good stuff in their lives and told me about the bad stuff instead. And hopefully one day, if things go spectacularly wrong, they will tell me first. I might go batshit crazy for a bit, but I will calm down and I will help them sort it out. Telling everyone you are OK is not always as brave as being honest.

There is a caveat to that of course. No one likes a moaner. If you have something trivial like a cold, sore throat or itchy leg, for God's sake keep it to yourself. No one has died. Suck it up.

5. If you have a perfect child, you are lucky. But sometimes you need a damaged one to realise it. I've had both. Two of my children were clearly seconds, but I am glad. It's good to be grateful your child can walk and talk. So many parents have perfectly healthy babies and just worry about trivial things instead. One thing you don't want to do in

life is fit in. The misfits are way more interesting to sit next to and won't be looking over your shoulder to see if there is someone more fabulous to talk to. As I tell my kids, it's good to be weird. All the best people are.

6. If you did something wrong, be there when it's put right – or as right as is possible. Even if you aren't wanted all the time. Acknowledging you feel guilty and maybe are guilty is fine. Deciding to take that bad feeling and use it to try to make amends is much, much better. I might have caused my daughter to be born without a hip because of my epilepsy medications, but I could certainly sleep beside her as we broke it and made it better.

CHAPTER 3

WHAT MADE YOU LIKE THIS?

I have been wondering how to get to the bit about what I actually do in life. Plenty of people ask: 'What do you do?' And there's no simple answer. So much of what I do rests on things I did before that I need to borrow your eyeballs and take them on a brief tour of my early adventures for you to get what my purpose is in life today.

The reason I do what I do, and the reason I am as I am, is because of everything I did back then. And my advice to anyone doing anything vaguely naughty or off-colour, anything that is not precisely according to the rule book or stuff your sensible mates would not approve of, is to do more of it while you can – much more.

If you are single, unmarried, between important jobs, a student at uni or somehow financing yourself but untied to anything significant like a person, a baby or a house, then for God's sake live big.

Say yes to everything, throw caution to the wind and sign up for stuff – accepting that if all goes horribly wrong, it's part

of the ride. A bit like going on a roller-coaster and chucking
up down your top. Own the fun and the consequences.

Don't listen to anyone from the Green Party, a militant wing
of the LGBT or boss-eyed feminists who think free-bleeding
is empowering. And for God's sake don't get involved in
charitable causes. Virtue is for the rich or the elderly. You are
neither. (In my day, one signalled impetigo or being an easy
lay; nowadays one signals virtue.)

There are some things you probably shouldn't do, of course.
So-called legal highs seem to be the opposite of a good idea,
given that so many young people who indulge in them are
found stone-cold dead in some godforsaken playground the
next morning. And I am not certain unprotected sex with
legions of men from Bumble, Tinder and other assorted
dating sites makes for much gynaecological sense. Sussing a
bloke out while absolutely blotto, in the dark and deafened
by the noise of a club, might not be highly effective as far as
sexual screening goes, but you can at least identify whether he
smells clean or has a group of mates, rather than being some
loner with chronic crabs and the ability to manipulate photos
online.

Chemsex also seems inherently flawed. My mate partied for
thirty-eight hours straight on chemicals and woke up with a
sweaty Iranian man taking him from behind while he slept. I
do not condone this kind of partying. And I hope my children
find fun that doesn't involve a syringe and endless willies.

But inside of healthy boundaries, and dependent on your
appetite for risk, if you are living life on the wild side, keep on
living it. The time for being sensible is long. And the impact

of having a child cannot be underestimated. You don't just give birth to a baby: you give birth to a gnawing guilt that penetrates your soul and takes effort to contain.

Just the other night I went out with a young woman in New York who had not been on a night out since her son was born. Her son is two.

If you are sitting reading this with an empty womb, and ovaries warming eggs, yet to be fertilised or hatched, for Christ's sake put this bloody book down and get out there. Run, walk naked down the road, go and drink four beers just because you can, arrange to meet your mate, go swimming, take a spin class – do anything. But don't sit in. Reading books is for when you are confined. By paralysis or by children.

The message I am trying to ram home is that the 'you' that emerges after a youth spent doing things you shouldn't may well be the foundation for, and what keeps you sane during, your future career.

I can honestly say I look back without a single regret. And am fairly proud that when my time comes I will have lived life sufficiently large.

The naughtier the thing, the more it makes me smile internally when some dullard from compliance is boring me about rules, or yet another man tells me 'no, you can't' or 'that was a bad decision'.

Frankly, being young and doing what everyone else was doing was making me slightly insane. After escaping the nuns at my school, I legged it to the biggest state comprehensive I could find. Two thousand students studying everything from advanced physics to car mechanics, on one sprawling campus.

The car mechanics would rev about the car park on their lunch break, and creative types studying some useless -ology or other would lie stoned on the grass in Dr Martens and goth-wear.

I was a little fish in a big pond. No differentiators save for a clutch of straight As and a couple of music Grade 8s. No significant markings. Nothing to separate me from the other 1,999 piling through the gates. Just one set of gates in a country full of school gates. And another kid trying to find a place and have someone to sit with at lunch.

Lesson: you aren't special at sixteen.

HOPKINS THE CULTURAL AMBASSADOR

At seventeen I left to spend a year in a school in Australia. Sent by the Rotary Club, I was supposed to be fostering relations between Australia and the UK. I am not certain I ever achieved this. In fact, my second host family, who I annoyed immensely, would probably go so far as to suggest I was about as welcome as the original British colonials.

But I did try to foster very special relations with a guy called Paul who already had a girlfriend and refused to be unfaithful. And I spent an enjoyable year at Pennant Hills High School dressed in the sort of uniform you see on *Home and Away*, with a zip up the back, a short skirt and an industrial-sized white collar like a landing pad for Martians. Funnily enough my own girls now have Australian uniforms at their thoroughly British private schools and it makes me laugh that their collars come down to their first rib and beyond.

It's strange to think I jetted off on my own at seventeen to stay with families I didn't know, attend a school I had never seen and become a speaker at conferences on the importance of Anglo-Australian relations. It's my most outstanding contribution to the Commonwealth to date. I look at my own eldest child, now thirteen, and wonder if I would allow her to go to the other side of the world, solo, in four years' time. I hope so. But I don't know so. And I now think seventeen is very young to be off on a one-way ticket to the other side of the world all alone. I will need to be braver for my own children.

By eighteen I was back at college finishing off my A-levels, with no friends and no crowd to call my own. I was the odd kid who had to start all over again, with a strong Australian accent and a sense of the world being bigger than the walk to the bus stop or the town centre, but I had an altogether better time standing alone than trying to fit in.

Lesson: fitting in with people whose biggest adventure is using a Topshop cubicle on their own is not important. Don't make school the only thing you do. Please be more interesting than three or four A-levels.

HOPKINS THE MUSIC TEACHER

After college, I buggered off on the road again to Pennsylvania to teach American kids music and drama at Camp America, an arts camp where American parents dumped their kids for an entire summer vacation so they didn't have to worry about childcare. Camps like these are the first stage of the long American ritual of parents investing heavily in their children. And American children being taught how to be self-confident and shine.

Equipped with Grade 8 violin and piano and a smile, plus

some attire that I imagined said 'music teacher' (floaty stuff with flowers on it and crap jewellery), I suddenly found myself in the middle of an American forest with art lessons to teach, musicals to stage and concerts to perform. Each camp counsellor slept in the children's accommodation. These were large wooden huts with twelve or so beds and a bathroom space shared with the sister hut that contained another twelve. My job outside of teaching hours was to keep these young Americans from misbehaving or feeling homesick or suicidal. It was quite a big brief for an eighteen-year-old without a clue.

My personal sub-brief was to have the maximum amount of fun possible, and encourage the kids on camp to do the same.

Once a week we had camp clean-up, during which all possessions, shoes and bedding were flung out the door while we gave the sleeping huts a good sweep, mop and scrub in order to stop us all from getting Ebola. This being America, competition was involved: one hut would be declared the winner. The exercise also allowed the camp managers to see which camp counsellors were made of the sort of American grit they needed, and to weed out the hopeless cases.

I used to love these days – just me and my little team of campers, sorting our stuff out and larking about together in the sun. Back then there was no such thing as internet, Wi-Fi or phones for kids. Life seemed far more simple, on reflection, and far better.

Once a week, staff were allowed to take the camp bus and bugger off for a day of frolicking about near lakes, eating crap at roadside diners, wearing small clothing and getting through as many beers as we could lay our hands on before having to return to our camp beds inside the children's huts without appearing too drunk to function.

Some of us pulled this off better than others. Others got sent home. One Irish lady, who was part of our reprehensible squad and a firm favourite of the groovy gang I was part of, failed spectacularly to meet camp standards. She was sacked for some minor misdemeanour or other, like half-killing a fat kid in her charge – or failing to at least pretend to be sober. In true student solidarity we sent a letter of protest to the Camp America management, to which we all added our signatures. We even faxed it from their office.

I didn't give the matter another moment's thought. It was, quite possibly, the first time I had raised my head above the parapet, or so much as waved in the face of power with a pen.

I signed that letter protesting about the treatment of our camp buddy and, for some reason, my name was the one that stood out.

It did not go down well.

During a violin lesson I was giving in a field outside the music hut (embracing how right-on you have to be to teach music), I saw the son of the camp boss in his golf buggy swerving violently towards me at high speed.

I can tell you this: a golf buggy can be driven in a way that clearly lets you know the driver is fuming, spitting mad. It is the opposite of the way a golf buggy is supposed to be driven, nonchalantly, by a large, wealthy, capitalist American in a pair of plus fours at the eighth, without a care in the world.

And sure enough, within moments the man was in my

face, waggling the letter with my signature into my over-sized nose, swearing at me for being a traitorous little British bitch who deserved to go the fuck home and shut the fuck up.

How the fuck dare I sign a letter complaining about the treatment of a stupid Irish woman at this fucking camp that belonged to his goddamn father, who I'd had the cheek to be nice to? A camp that had paid to drag my sorry arse from England, for all the fucking gratitude I had shown.

And on he went. And on and on.

I was standing, holding a violin, next to a seven-year-old girl. I asked her politely to excuse us and wait inside the music hut. I asked him if we could continue our conversation in one moment. And he stormed off.

It is perhaps my earliest memory of standing up for something on my own, outside of my family, and watching someone detonate in my face. And knowing at the same time I needed to look like I was in control, for the sake of my little camper waiting inside.

It's almost like being an outside observer in your own conflict. You remove the emotion and listen dispassionately. And weirdly enough, you stop noticing the noise and the angry words, and see the small stuff instead, like the amount of spit that flies out the side of their mouth. Or how many blackheads they have in their ear. I still remember the blackheads in his ear.

I learned two things. First, allowing someone to vent makes them feel better and, taken the right way, doesn't make you feel any worse.

Second, watching someone drive a golf buggy in a temper is pretty funny.

It wasn't until he came and apologised later that it struck me that, as a thirty-something male, he probably shouldn't have been screaming swear words at a teenage girl standing in a field trying to teach a seven-year-old kid (paying full fees) to play the violin.

It was the first time I had ever been properly shouted at by a fully grown adult in a work setting. And it would not be the last. The media industry is full of angry men who have been known to swear in my face. That happened again only yesterday, and *that* won't be the last time either.

These things make us stronger.

Lesson: if someone is shouting at you, imagine you are watching from above, like an angel on the ceiling. And focus on something small on their face, like a spot. Or their ear hair.

My saddest memory of that American summer camp is that some of the kids sent to us for the full six weeks were only six years old. I was there for two six-week blocks. On the day the parents came to collect their most precious little people, inevitably many were late. And one forgot their kid altogether. I remember sitting with her while the office tried to track down her parents and all of us counsellors tried to keep her mind off the thing the rest of us were thinking: that her parents were utter bastards.

Lesson: being a bit rubbish at being a mum is one thing. I am a self-confessed crap mum. But failing to collect your child after a six-week stint away is pretty damn low. If you have a kid, buy a calendar.

Other parents were freaky. One dad took a 'special' shine to me when he was dropping off his daughter (only eight years my junior) and sent me endless letters, each more persuasive than the last, offering to take me out in the hills in his soft-top car and give me the sort of day I would never forget. I decided he could forget the day he was never going to have, and stopped replying.

Lesson: just because dads have kids, it doesn't mean they think with their hearts or heads. Their balls still call the shots. And some dads are weird.

Looking back, a 45-year-old man trying to hit on the teen-age camp counsellor of his daughter's arts camp is pretty sick. And the things he offered to do to me halfway up a hill in Pennsylvania in the back of his soft-top, even more so.

And bear in mind I was dressed like a vapid, quinoa-eating vegan who taught music at band camp, and probably looked like I recycled my own Tampax. I was not the vision of beauty that you see on this cover today… although, arguably, now I look more like a lesbian bookseller than ever.

I never saw that kid's dad again. But I always felt differently about his daughter – kind of sorry for her, I think, that her dad was a greaseball and not at all like my dad at home, who could be trusted in a room full of naked and nubile young women to ask only for a cup of tea with not too much milk; who would drink it and then tell you 'it's all pouring out my head' as he sweated on the sofa.

While that dad was rejected, another guy, Mark – also out from the UK to teach sports – was my official camp crush. I say crush, but I can still remember the way my entire summer pivoted around that one boy. He made Camp America. He *was* that summer.

Frustratingly, he had a girlfriend and refused to be unfaithful. I spent the summer trying to get him to do bad things to me – casually, without him actually noticing. We took out our sexual frustration in wrestling matches, which were as close to physical contact as I could get without him having to remind me he was taken.

He taught football and had great legs and calves the size of Cornish bullocks in football socks – a fact he was acutely aware of and never ceased to exploit. He had twelve weeks of unadulterated American summer in which to do bad things to me, and he failed to acquiesce. Twelve weeks! That's longer than it takes a rabbit to give birth and raise a brood. Twice.

God only knows where we would have actually done the dark deed, given that we both shared our huts with twelve American kids under fourteen. But if he'd had the will, I'd have found a way.

I had never known a boy quite like him. And I can't say I have since.

Typically, the moment I returned to university halls – day two, week one, term one – with new mates, new people, new faces, a whole new life to be getting on with, guess who showed up? Bloody Camp America Mark, expecting me to fall at his feet. Plonker!

He had got home, realised his girlfriend was a complete doughnut compared to my splendid self (apologies to that girl; he said it, not me), and thought now would be a good time to consummate twelve weeks of longing in the forest.

Arsehole.

Lesson: being faithful is an excellent idea if you are married. Being overly faithful when you are seventeen is nonsense. It's the equivalent of going to an all-inclusive buffet and only eating a ham sandwich. (I regret that analogy already.)

I sent him back to the train station with a frown. Men should realise: some of them are for a lifetime, some are for a short time, and some have a window. He had a window and that window was now closed.

It's strange, given I am certainly not a looker. And it was perfectly clear to me from an early age who the beautiful girls were, and how the boys just fell about near them.

And yet, girls like me aren't available for long, and tend to have more boyfriends than time on their hands. I have been in relationships since I was fourteen and never really been single.

If the free market teaches you anything, it's that fun, sporty girls who don't take themselves too seriously and are prepared to put out pretty athletically but don't ask for any emotional reassurance outside of the private time you spend together are fairly thin on the ground. We are in limited supply.

HOPKINS THE SEX THERAPIST

Given that you have forked out a fiver or more for this book, I should tell you the truth: I did go to meet Camp America Mark at his university, in the digs he shared with his footie mates. I had decided we should have sex once just to put the matter to bed, so to speak. And quite possibly because I wanted the final word over the irritating girlfriend he had insisted on being faithful to for so long.

This time it was my turn to learn a nasty lesson: some things are best left unfinished.

Not only did Mark have a micro penis that was about as effective as a straw in a large American milkshake glass, but he was also a premie. I have never met one before or since. And I have no intention of meeting one ever again. Not a premature baby, you understand. That would be weird. A premature ejaculator.

All of a whirl, he got out his straw, dipped it into my full American milkshake and shouted: 'DON'T MOVE. DON'T MOVE. NO! NO!'

I froze, imagining for a moment that a large tarantula had crawled across the bed towards my head and was about to launch a deadly strike on my eyeball – which would have been awkward enough – or that armed men had just burst in behind me and were about to shoot me at point-blank range. That might, in fact, have been a blessed relief and saved me from actually dying of embarrassment.

But then he juddered. I felt a familiar warm sensation oozing down my inner thigh and realised the micro penis had delivered its micro load; the delivery driver was face down on the pillow, mortified.

You might imagine monster Hopkins – telling it like it is – would get up, give him a good kicking and tell him to man the fuck up and stop acting like a teen with acne. I kind of wish I had.

What I did was far worse.

I told him it was no big deal and perfectly understanda-ble. That it was probably all a bit too much excitement after so much anticipation, and didn't matter at all. And I politely stayed the night like it was fine. I was even kind and affectionate. Well, as much as you can be with a man who has a micro penis.

Next morning I kissed and comforted him like I was his bloody mother, made him feel better about himself (the utter moron) and legged it back to university knowing I would never EVER see him again.

Lesson: when confronted by a micro penis, best just to call it early.

Like this: 'Sorry, Mark. That thing is going to get lost in my thing. It's not that you're small. It's that I'm massive. It would be like reversing a Mini into the Mersey Tunnel. Let's go for a beer instead.'

Do not wait, try to bluff your way through it as best you can, and then waste the next ten hours trying to make some half-man feel better. At seventeen, you've got far better ways to fill your time.

It's why I always worry for these women who don't have sex until their wedding night. I understand the excitement factor, and completely buy into how romantic it all sounds. I mean, in an age when everything is on tap, when we can arrange anonymous sex on Tinder with strangers we will never see again, what could be more romantic than waiting until your wedding night to let your new hubby poke his trouser snake into your rabbit burrow? (Actually, mine is more like a rabbit warren; but I digress.)

American girls, particularly those in NYC, love this whole waiting-until-your-wedding-night lark, working on the basis that it helps crowbar a diamond onto their finger faster because their bloke is so desperate for a lay he thinks it might hurry it along.

In truth, though, the things that matter in life need to be tested rigorously. And if we are thinking about keeping them for a long time, they need to be road-tested. This is why we test-drive cars and look around new houses a few times before we put in an offer: we need to be sure about what we are taking on.

You need to know you are marrying someone with a micro penis who only manages a brief judder before blowing his tiny load BEFORE that ring goes on your finger. And the engagement ring better make it damn well worth it if you decide to go ahead.

I have a theory that the size of the diamond in your ring may be inversely related to the size of your future husband's penis: the dodgier the penis, the bigger the rock. It would explain a great deal about Kanye West, his issues, and the size of Kim's five-carat ring.

I pitched this hypothesis on Twitter and, while many demanded that I demonstrate how I had formulated my theory ('show working out'), one man gave me anecdotal evidence in support of it: 'My wife's [diamond] is minuscule. Can hardly see it. Need a microscope.'

He is my kind of man, and clearly well-hung and should be celebrated as such.

There has been a second faulty penis episode in my life, but to be fair to its owner, who was, and no doubt still is, every inch an adorable person, I was never his type and I have no wish to embarrass him.

The poor lad was so desperate to prove to his parents that he was as straight as every other Welsh boy in the village, he adopted me as his girlfriend. He even took me home to introduce me to his ma and pa to prove the point.

As far as I could make out they were all related to each other and all lived on the same road. And everyone was expected to be married by eighteen and have two kids a year later. That was the system.

I learned two valuable things: 1) the Welsh for cuddle is cwtch; and 2) a cwtch from this lovely boy was about the loveliest thing going.

I still think he is brilliant for doing what he did – even though I was sort of used as a prop.

Funny thing is, he would never have needed to pretend to be straight for this whole thing to have worked. He could have told me he was gay and I would quite happily have gone along with the ruse if it kept his parents happy and made his life easier.

He was just a lovely boy, trying to please his ma and pa and all of his aunts and uncles who lived on the next road but one, wanting to be accepted like everyone else. If I was a small part of that, even for a moment, then I am delighted. I am sure by now he is out and proud, podium-dancing in sequinned hot pants to Kylie with the best of them.

Lesson: if your boyfriend turns out to be gay, it's not you, it's his mum. And his mum only wants what's best for him. As do you. So you all have a lot more in common than you think. Plus, gay boyfriends are epic. All the laughs and none of the massive effort of shaving your legs or waxing your bits.

In truth, all these adventures with boys and jobs were my real life at university. Being part of the University Officer Training Corps, running, working and boys were the core of my curriculum.

Uni itself was only ever a place in between other places for me. I cracked on. I had good mates, struggled over Economics, raged through the tedium of Statistics and flew through Politics. And was curiously brilliant at Public Policy Administration, which everyone else hated and was shit at.

Perhaps that was my true calling. Imagine that: hello, my name is Katie Hopkins and I work in public policy and administration.

Dear Jesus. What would I look like, I wonder? Shoulder-length brown hair, no makeup and a corduroy skirt, I shouldn't wonder, with those weird hand-made leather shoes in plum with a round toe and one buckle. How different my life would be.

If I really am so bloody interesting, which clearly I believe to be the case, how come I was so sodding spectacular at Public Policy Administration? I hate that kind of self-awareness. It's a bit like the fact that my hair is actually mousey brown. What the hell's that all about? Mousey. A less appropriate word for me would be pretty hard to find. And yet it's the colour of my hair, which comes out of my actual head.

Despite being unexpectedly genius at PPA, I was singularly awful at Economics and struggled monumentally with anything involving a graph. In order to pass Statistics, I had to learn the entire syllabus by rote.

I still maintain Economics is what happens when you put

men in charge of anything. None of them knows the right answer, none of them is willing to concede to the other, and no one is prepared to admit when they got it wrong.

Economics is essentially wild guesswork articulated as authoritatively as is humanly possible in order to convince the maximum number of people you are right.

It helps to be good-looking to achieve this. Mark Carney, the Governor of the Bank of England is a perfect example.

When he talks, legions of men and women are so preoccupied wondering just how good he smells naked, he could tell us he is increasing interest rates to 4.5 per cent and we would nod compliantly.

HOPKINS THE BARMAID/CLEANER

In order to take a breather from endless economics, when term ended, my itchy bones took me to Lundy Island in the English Channel for a summer job. I don't believe there was an official job title, but General Skivvy summarised it pretty well.

I remember catching the ferry early in the morning from the quay at Bideford, unexpectedly finding myself travelling with another lad also destined for an interview with the landlady of Lundy Island's pub. The advertisement was for a waiter, cleaner and general handyperson to live and work on the island. And we both had our bags packed for the season.

I didn't know it, but there was only one job going. A little later on in the day, having been told I had got the job, I saw my travel companion troop back down the hill to the boat to go home with his bag. I figured that would be a hard journey for him, and thought that I wouldn't much like to fail a job interview and be sent home.

Little did I know, back then, that this ruthless dispatch of individuals with their bags, all vying for one job, would be the thing that ended up setting my direction of travel for much of my adult life. Lundy was a mini-*Apprentice*. And I got the job.

That summer on Lundy Island was a formative one. I had my own little cottage to sleep in and about five different bits of clothing in my rucksack, and I was on my own on the island with only seventeen locals and a few thousand puffins.

I cleared up the pub first thing, went cleaning around the island's cottages on changeover days, and then returned to the pub to waitress lunch and dinner. I was also the queen of starters and puddings and, later, king of scrubbing and washing up.

It was not glamorous. But a steady flow of visitors and hardy, outdoorsy types kept the pub full and me busy.

In the pub I was pretty handy to have around. I could have a laugh with the visitors, sort their orders, pull pints and make food with the best of them.

Cleaning, on the other hand, was not my strength. The head cleaner was a frightfully posh woman with the demeanour of an ultra-strict matron on a Victorian ward. She was perfect for her job. I was not. She wanted everything spotless and pristine according to the exacting standards that were expected by the rather posh people who tended to book these sorts of properties on random islands in the English Channel. I wanted to get back to my job among the people and the pub.

I didn't fully appreciate it back then, but the Landmark Trust that ran the properties on Lundy Island typically catered for what I would now call the 'Islington Right-On Brigade'. These days I imagine they are the crusty vegan types who are heavily into green energy and probably recycle their tea bags.

The head cleaner instructed me, at length, on what was expected when cleaning a property, and I can remember thinking I should pretend to be interested even though I couldn't have been less interested if I'd tried.

I can still see her now, walking me through the phases of a clean, demonstrating the things to check for, showing me how to hoover down the back of the sofa and wash every dish in the cupboard. And I remember thinking she was utterly off her rocker if she thought all that was really necessary just for a few people to have a kip in a cottage for a few nights.

This became abundantly apparent when she came to inspect the first cottage she'd left me to clean. I had failed to check any of the 450,000 bits and pieces she had instructed me to check. The plates in the cupboard needed washing, the pots and pans hadn't been scrubbed, the bedrooms needed this or that, the floor was still dirty, and the cushions hadn't been taken off the sofa and plumped to her liking.

She told me that I had done a lousy job and was never going to make it as a cleaner. I was surprised because no one had ever really told me I was useless before, but then I figured she had a point. When she had left me to clean, I had had a little kip in the bed instead.

And so her criticism was, at worst, fair. And at best, pretty damn kind.

I remember walking away from that dirty cottage feeling kind of alright about the whole incident because I'd much rather be back working in the pub and having a laugh than changing poxy beds and scrubbing other people's dirty dishes.

That day, I made a commitment to myself that I would do whatever I had to do to please her and our guests, while expending the very minimum of effort on my part. It was my survival strategy for the summer.

Lesson: some things you do when you are young are inexcusable. And the best advice I have is not to fess up to them in a book that you openly encourage others to read. I could apologise to my former employers here. But that would be disingenuous. I worked like a little Trojan that summer, and the fact that I was a bit shit at cleaning is neither here nor there.

I called this special cleaning technique Hopkins Magic. It was magic in the sense that no cleaning had actually been done, but I hoped to give the illusion that the cottage was clean. Like really bad magic.

HOPKINS MAGIC
1. BEDDING
Changing the bedding after one night's stay makes no sense. It's completely irrational. Only a muppet would go through the major upheaval of stripping and remaking a double bed when they could quite easily get away with not doing so.

I see this as my one and quite possibly only contribution to the green movement, in that I conserved energy and water by merely *freshening* the bed.

Bed freshening involves changing pillow cases, hoovering the bed for pubes/toenails, checking for dodgy stains and damp patches, and then remaking it all by pulling all the sheets as tight as an accountant at a bar – so tight that a ball can bounce off the bloody thing. Maybe even consider ironing the bed sheet at the pillow end to give the impression of it having been laundered. Apply the clean pillows, add a little distraction to the bed – a flower, maybe, or a chocolate – and boom. Happy campers, minimum effort.

2. MUGS AND GLASSES

People often leave their mugs and glasses to be washed up by someone else. Your best hope is that they were never washed up by me. They never saw water. Only a good wipe with the former guests' bathroom towels.

It haunts me to this day whenever I stay in a hotel – and I stay in many. If you are of a sensitive disposition or in the slightest bit OCD about things being clean or at least sanitary, I advise you to look away now.

In fact, best skip to the next chapter and pretend this one ends here.

This is why, even now, I can't use a hotel mug today without washing it first. I do see that I have brought this on myself.

I have mates who work in some of the large budget hotel chains who confirm that the real purpose of the miniature kettle is to act as a bed pan for the lads who can't be arsed to make it to the toilet. And more often than not, they are filled with piss, not water, when they come to clean. And the remote control has more faecal matter on it than a children's soft-play centre at McDonald's.

Really, the reception desk at budget hotel chains should hand over anti-bacterial wipes with every room key, so you can de-faecal the things you are going to touch.

Cleaning aside, I loved my job as the bar girl of the island. And when the pub landlords took an extended vacation from the island, I took over the pub, ordering, changing barrels and keeping things ticking along.

Before too long Chris, the trusty island handyman, had become the object of my undying affection. I am not certain he had ever learned to read or write, and I suspect a noxious cocktail of toxic drugs taken throughout his teenage years had addled his brain. But my desire for Chris was never about what he wasn't, but what he was.

He was a rudimentary man – and a good-looking rudimentary man at that. You know the hot felon that was all over the news? The one that was snogging Philip Green's daughter on his yacht? With the cheekbones you could cut your finger on? Well, he reminds me of Chris.

Naked save for a big boiler suit and a massive pair of pull-on Dockers boots like they wear on an oil rig, Chris banged around that island on his quad bike fixing, mending, repairing and herding.

Skin-headed, tanned, tattooed and naked. DID I MENTION HE WAS NAKED? Chris *was* Lundy for me.

I even returned in the Christmas holidays to carry on our fling. But it wasn't the same then; it was cold, the island was small and isolated, and Chris just seemed like a stupid bloke in overalls. I would never get back that summer when I was the bar girl of Lundy Island.

Lesson: never return. If you have great memories that make your heart sing, don't contaminate them, or mute them, by trying to live them again.

I don't go back to anything in life now. I imagine myself like a ship's bow, or an arrow in the wind, or my daughter diving into the pool like a little sea lion: streamlined and forward-moving. When the incoming attacks get particularly harsh, I tuck my head in and visualise the arrow head shooting on by, leaving behind the past and all the surrounding noise.

This episode explains why I don't like to apologise when I have said something to which people have taken offence. Apologising involves trying to go back and correct the past. And no one can do that except in the movies. You can only hope to do better moving forwards.

Apologising never actually stops people complaining anyway. The apology is never enough – or never soon enough, or never sincere enough. And they will be right, you are only apologising because you had to – so what the hell's the point?

It also explains why I have never met up with the teams involved in *The Apprentice*, *Big Brother* or any other series after filming has ended. Why I don't go back to school reunions. Why I haven't made contact with solid mates from my job with my first husband. Because I think things that are done should be left where they were, and I'm wary of raking up old hurt or spoiling the thing as I remembered it.

I watched my son swimming in a race the other day, a race he was winning. But every few strokes he kept looking behind to see how close his mate was and to suss out whether he could stay ahead.

When I went off to Sandhurst in my army years, I used to be their 800-metre runner. I can remember the PT instructor issuing me one of the biggest bollockings of my military running career for daring to glance back to see whether I was going to win the damn race. You face the line and you run to it. Never look back. You are only beaten by things that are in front of you. He was right. And it's something I'd encourage others to learn.

Lesson: don't be beaten by things that are behind you. If you have done something truly dreadful, or humiliated yourself to the point you feel physically sick (me, often), then make peace with yourself. Don't take the nightmare with you. Accept that you are allowed to screw up big time and leave it there, in the past.

Don't try to go back and hold onto memories. Or relive good times. Let old nightmares rest. Let beautiful dreams sleep sweetly. Keep moving forward towards the line.

HOPKINS THE SECURITY GUARD

Next up on my list of adventures to distract myself from the fact that university was highly overrated and bloody dull and way too long for any vaguely interesting individual was a summer working at Disneyland Paris.

I decided that France could do with a piece of me, and I remember turning up for training somewhere in Paris and standing on a chair cheering as part of some cringe-worthy team-building exercise.

Most other sensible university types were dressed like students and scruffy as hell. For reasons unclear to me now, I decided to go the full job-interview effort and rocked up in a blazer and long skirt looking like the Conservative candidate for Richmond.

I am certain all the other kids there thought I was a complete plonker, but thanks to my military blazer and my ability to fake a level of competence in French that I didn't actually possess, I was processed off to join security.

Others went to food, guest relations and arrivals, all of which were mind-numbingly dull and resulted in them heading for home a few weeks into the job.

Life as a security officer in Disneyland Paris, on the other hand, was pretty darn epic. Each morning you would collect your 'costume' from a huge uniform store backstage, cleaned, ironed and pressed for purpose, before you joined your team and got to work.

The company that organised all the security staff uniforms and feeding was called Sodexo – amazingly, the same company that provide private prisons in the UK – I like to think I have a fall-back career with them if I fancy it.

My security shift was from 2 p.m. to park closing at 11 p.m., which meant I was part of the team responsible for clearing the park at night. This meant chasing the druggies out of the caves in the Pirates of the Caribbean, and the hash smokers out of Space Mountain.

There are plenty of places to hide if you know Disneyland well.

I got to waft about the park looking like some kind of real security authority in a lookie-likey police uniform with a walkie-talkie on my belt, big black boots and tight trousers… and I loved it.

At Disney, where dreams come true, the boys and girls who were never good enough to join the actual military or police were keeping their own dreams alive by playing Cagney and Lacey for a day job. They even had a code for stuff that went on in the park:

Dix-quatre: 'understood'. Dix-soixante: 'yes'. Dix-trois: 'help'.

There were codes for fights, for ambulances, for violent assault and for urgent back-up. Codes for lost children and drunk children. And codes for fat people who had passed out next to their wheelchairs. And codes for a dead body on a ride.

Every kind of madness that could happen in a theme park was coded into radio speak and we merry band of brave pretend-security lunatics would be right there on receive, ready to save the day.

I was suitably over-dramatic at all times and was criticised heavily as such by the old men of the unit. I called for more ambulances and emergency back-up over that one summer season than were called out during the rest of the year put together.

If someone fell, my immediate judgement would be that they had broken a leg. If a fat person passed out in the heat, I would call in a heart attack.

This was primarily the result of two things, the first of which was a failure to understand how much people like to moan. People like to moan a lot.

When a tourist falls down a bank and lands awkwardly, they don't just grunt a bit and get out of there as soon as they can to try to survive the shame. *Non. Zut alors!* They flail about like a helpless stuck pig in a hole, squealing like they're in agony and leading me, a twenty-year-old pretend-security guard, to report that they were in grave mortal danger, even though it usually turned out that most of them had nothing more than a splinter.

Second, I had never before seen so many grossly unfit people in one place. Watching a chubster collapse under the sheer weight of their own body after loading up on two family-fun bucket-meals and eight litres of full-fat coke is a marginally terrifying thing. Especially if they topple sideways out of their electric wheelchair and lie motionless on the deck, softly leaking.

I would shriek and run to the person in a way I thought security guards should run, yelling into my radio for an ambulance, shouting the code for heart attack and my location, only to find that Fat Lynda was just taking a breather before beginning the arduous job of moving one leg.

Seriously. It's not that I dislike fat people. I just don't trust them to actually be OK, to the extent that if they faint in the heat and the crowds, I assume their body has quite naturally given up the fight for life.

And I can tell you, Disneyland is a magnet for the least active, the monumentally stupid and the downright morbidly obese, who love nothing more than to drive up, stand on the moving escalator to the entrance, hit a mobility scooter and queue all day eating themed crap. That is their dream, and for sixty or so quid a day Disney makes it come true.

The list of mad things that can happen in the park is truly endless. Unsurprisingly, paedophiles love the place. If your thing is distracted young children, then Disneyland is the Mecca of your perversion. I plucked a paedo wearing only a boiler suit with an especially low zip out of the Peter Pan maze where he was flashing young girls.

I noted, on the paperwork I was obliged to file, that his penis looked flaccid and small. My boss made me delete that bit, as if it was an affront to French men from a British woman.

Finding lost children at the park was a never-ending job, like scooping up penguins after they have smelled fish. There was a special holding pen for them – dix-vingt: 'lost child' – and paperwork to be completed to ensure they weren't whisked away by a passing paedo before some mildly hysterical parents came to retrieve them, crushing your bones with their gratitude and relief. I get it. If I lost a kid at Disney I would go out of my mind with fear. But probably more scary was that hugely unqualified kids like me had been employed as 'security'.

I was inept at wrangling children, and equally inept, if not more so, at the car park patrols. One job was patrolling the endless car park for dogs or babies locked in cars. Or for thieves. The other was driving guests around in the golf cart while they repeatedly pressed their key fob to try to find their car.

My own father lost the family car when we went to Disney as kids – so I get that it is easily done. And driving a golf cart about dressed as a security guard while not actually giving a crap is a pretty good holiday job by anyone's standards. Especially when you have been a cleaner on an island.

On one car park patrol, adopting my character as Security Special Op-Hopkins, I found a car with one of our parking cones unceremoniously shoved under each back wheel. Tut-tutting at this clear violation of Disneyland etiquette, I removed the cones and went about my jolly important task of being jolly important in a uniform, with a radio. And tight trousers.

Next day at the shift briefing, our head of department ran through the outstanding notices and updates we all needed to know. One was the alarming news that there had been an attack on the car park resulting in a crash and damage to two parked vehicles.

It seemed that during the attack some gutless thug had removed vital safety cones that were being used as a car's brake system after the failure of the handbrake. Said car had rolled back and slammed into another car, rendering both stuck in Disneyland and the owner threatening to sue.

I sank down in my chair and tried to look fiercely disapproving and not at all guilty. This is a tricky look to pull off, especially when you have clearly been the cause of a major car crash in car park three, section delta.

Lesson: don't interfere in matters that don't concern you. Just because you are dressed as one thing, or have a title, doesn't mean anything. It is called a costume and a title. A uniform, some character acting and a walkie-talkie – that's all it took for people to believe I would save or help them. In fact,

I crashed their cars and called in fainting fat people as heart attacks and strokes.

As with every holiday job, there was, inevitably, a man involved. This time it was Francois, who was ex-military and looked like a real policeman even though he wasn't.

Wise old me now knows to give an extremely wide berth to any grown man who still works as a security guard in a theme park as his full-time career. And effectively wears a costume to work. Young me saw the military in him, revelled in his manliness, and was fairly excited about the way he spoke French in a whisper.

He was a good teacher and a kind one. And, given my limited ability to speak the language, I may well have been a far more enjoyable companion back then than my husband endures today.

Francois and I spent a happy summer together, staying in his tiny flat in Paris, having coffee and croissants on the way to work in the day, pretending to be security guards by night.

My final adventure before conceding that I might actually have to crack on with life and get on with my proper job of passing officer training and becoming the first British female general, was to backpack around southern Africa and Indonesia with my army mate Neil.

HOPKINS THE BUDGET BACKPACKER

Neil and I were properly best mates: we liked running about, having sex when drunk then pretending we never had, competing at press-ups and sit-ups and generally doing anything physical that hurt a lot. My nickname for him was Nails – as in hard as – and later Steel – as in Steely Neily. You get the idea. To me, he was invincible.

His father was ex-military, he was always destined to be SAS and despite not being conventionally good-looking, girls seemed to fall about wherever he stood.

Neil and I did backpacking properly – surviving on just a couple of pounds a day, we thumbed rides, caught local boats to see Komodo dragons and borrowed snorkel kits from kids to explore the coral reefs.

Six weeks into backpacking around Indonesia, bitten to infinity by a legion of mosquitoes, sleeping wherever *Lonely Planet* or some random local advised, we looked considerably less sturdy than when we left.

We slept in dirty beds with no air con or mozzie nets, hadn't washed properly in weeks and ate way too much dodgy pad thai. Drinking the local tap water and putting all our young faith in sterilising tablets hadn't helped our situation either.

We both had full-scale dysentery. We vomited and shat our way through a week of hell. We've all been there, so caught between needing to shit and to vomit that you need two places: the toilet and bath combo, or the toilet and bucket combo.

Now, remove the bath and bucket and add another fully grown human, a humidity of eighty, temperatures of 92 degrees, and a plague of mosquitoes to the scenario, and you have a week of Neil and me backpacking – or rather, performing synchronised shitting – around Indonesia.

Neil was too sick to move, so I would hobble to the local shed that sold stuff to beg them for the sealed bottled water, not the stuff they had been refilling from the tap. In hand gestures.

I am not sure if the gesture for 'stop killing us with your shady tap water, you little bastards' is internationally recognised. But I made myself clear.

We recovered. But I do wonder what might have happened if we hadn't. Or if we had got worse, not better. No one knew where we were, or had reason to care, or expected us anywhere. I wonder, if we had both died in the night, how long would it have taken for anyone to notice. Presumably once the smell and the flies had got beyond a point even locals hardened to the third world could withstand.

And I also see how not having mobile phones, and your family not expecting to hear from you from one month to the next, can actually be pretty good things. Your family don't worry about you because they are not expecting to hear from you.

And far from calling for help at the first sign of disaster, you are compelled to try to cope.

I had never really noticed being a white girl that much before. But outside central Jakarta I was a freak. A blonde, pale-skinned oddity towering over everyone, schlepping about with a tatty bag on her back, trailing a miserable-looking bloke with a sore arse.

Bending over to get in the back of a minibus through the rear doors, one of the men from the eternal gaggle staring at us British curiosities got a bit too bold and inserted an index finger up my foof.

I sat down quickly and shut up.

I never told Neil. I never told anyone. And I never thought too much more about it other than being shocked it had happened and wondering if it did really happen, and why a bloke would shove a finger up your foof just for fun. Out of context. When all you were trying to do was get in his van.

I figured out pretty fast it meant I needed to be more careful when bending over. And I never again got on transport without Neil right behind me on that trip. And I got a swift lesson in how some men see women. Neil saw me as his partner and his mate. That filthy freak saw me as a vagina he might be able to poke his finger into.

But it's a strange thing. When I think of Indonesia, I remember it as an adventure in its truest sense: brave, rough, hand-to-mouth, without plan or care. Proper backpacking. I remember snorkelling with locals wearing a dodgy mask. I remember Komodo dragons and the heat and the taste of Jungle Formula and itchy mozzie bites. And being on the edge of paradise, without all the idiocy of Western frills and nonsense.

And this memory of the man who put his finger in me is right there. It is sharp and vivid. Like a rock in the sand. It has stayed with me.

Our journey around southern Africa was also on the rough side of life. We stayed in Johannesburg and travelled through Bulawayo, two of the most dangerous cities in the world. Our plan was to see Zambia and the waterfalls, then catch public transport down to Cape Town.

One night we caught a sleeper train. There were six little bunks in our cabin, a stack of three on each side. Neil and I took a bed each, and each of the other beds held a family of four. Eighteen of us, in a cabin for six. And we were in the posh bit of the train.

Eight hours later we were woken up and told to get off. I

assumed we had arrived. I did remember hearing a big thud in the night, and a few locals opposite being thrown from their bunks, but I'd assumed the driver was a bit heavy-footed with the old brakes.

We found ourselves standing in the middle of a field, in the middle of nowhere. We hadn't gone anywhere – eight hours of travelling to cover an hour's worth of distance. And there on the tracks was a dead elephant.

A dead elephant! Positively real compared to whatever crap we are fed when our British trains are delayed and the announcer presses the excuse randomiser for us muppets on the platform. Signal failure. Or the late arrival of the catering crew. Or the wrong kind of rain.

Abandoned in the early dawn on the trackside somewhere outside of Johannesburg, we were on our own again.

Replacement bus services aren't a thing in Africa. Nor is complaining to someone imagining they will help you. It's far more linear: this happened. Now this has happened. Now there is no train. End of.

An elephant was on the tracks. An elephant had died. So did the train. So get off.

So we stuck out our thumbs and started walking along the road south, and hitchhiked our way to the next somewhere. I think back to that girl I was. And I see now that she was pretty fearless, even back then.

I was nineteen, Neil twenty. When I look around at nineteen-year-olds these days being dropped at train stations, tickets bought by mummy, daddy at the other end to collect them, carrying phones, clothes, money, all provided by the

Bank of Mum and Dad, I see how far we have gone in a generation. It isn't progress.

We survived hitchhiking. We were picked up by a lovely man called Joseph and went on our merry way. Looking back, I think we were lucky. Would I do this again now? Probably not.

Lesson: you are young. Say yes before you learn to be scared and say no. And when things go a bit pear-shaped, don't grab your phone and ring your parents. Or tweet the customer service department of some firm. Perhaps the thing to do is see if you can solve things for yourself. Think, 'What Would Katie Hopkins Do?' (Then laugh.) That's what we used to do and it worked pretty darn well.

Lesson: life doesn't follow a straight path. You may plan your destination and your journey, but things change – some inside of your control, some outside (like dysentery, or an elephant on the tracks). You may have signed up for a three-year degree, but that's just your baseline activity. Real life is out there, waiting for you to really learn it. The important thing is to be brave, or at least to pretend to be, to course correct, and to keep moving forwards. Sometimes you have to go sideways before you can move up. And that's OK too.

Finally, equipped with all of these lessons from my holiday jobs and a shabby 2:1 in Economics and Politics, I headed off to begin my formal training as an officer in the British Army, destined for the Intelligence Corps. I packed my bags and my ironing board and was dropped off on the parade square of the Royal Military Academy Sandhurst. Things had just got real.

CHAPTER 4

EPILEPSY AND ME

It's a bit odd sitting here writing about my epilepsy – something I didn't talk about for twenty years suddenly appearing full frontal on the page.

It makes me feel a bit like I just walked into a hotel lobby naked in the middle of the day without realising, exposing myself unnecessarily, a streaker in my own book.

Even after beating the damn thing, I am embarrassed by it. I feel that epilepsy made me weaker. When people are kind enough to book me a train ticket, I don't tell them I have a disabled card because I don't want them to think less of me or to think I am not strong.

That seems like a terrible thing to write, inferring that I think other disabled people are weak. But that isn't it. I am not talking about you over there being brave with your disability. Or you in the corner, registered disabled, trying not to take offence.

It is common these days for people to speak 'on behalf of'. Lily Allen, for example, apologised for Britain. Madonna's kid Lourdes spoke 'on behalf of' America.

I don't claim to represent anything or anyone – not

epileptics, nor the registered disabled, even if we share the same ordeal of the same stuff. We probably have things in common, or understand each other well, but I know I don't represent anyone.

I am talking about me. This is how I feel – the whole muddled horrible lot of it. It's about not wanting people to think differently about my ability to commit to stuff just because of something I cannot change. And I think that is something we all share.

I know every day is a battle for thousands of people out there. For too many, just walking down the stairs, taking a bath, getting public transport or being alone among strangers takes real courage.

And the only thing that makes you want to cry about how hard this can be is all the other people out there who do all that without even having to think about it. To them all that stuff is trivial, the reflex of life – the nothing on which you layer your everything.

The upsetting bit is not that others take it for granted. They should. I would. You never wish that other people should suffer to make you feel better. This is not about wanting other people to struggle or feel worse. You don't need someone else to be suffering more… (And if you do then you need to go and sit in a corner and have a bloody word with yourself.) Everyone should take walking down the stairs or having a bath for granted. My kids do, and I couldn't be gladder for them.

The thing that gnaws away at you is the fact that you can't, and that these ordinary things take up so much head space. So much of what you might usefully apply to exciting stuff, or profitable stuff, or happy stuff is used up with nonsense. You go to bed hoping the night won't be too dreadful, that you won't have a major fit, that you will wake up with your arms in their sockets and with a tongue that hasn't been bitten into such a bloody pulp that you sound like a deaf person when you speak.

I remember all the times I had to do radio interviews on the telephone, desperately over-enunciating so they wouldn't hear my bloodied tongue missing syllables, taking paracetamol to numb the pain of talking.

I had extreme fits for about ten years. Speaking honestly, given I am standing naked in front of you, those ten years, from the age of thirty to forty, had been more than a rough ride. And I'd had enough. I was ready to fall asleep and not wake up, or at least, more than ready to not wake up with two dislocated arms, a bloodied tongue and not knowing my own name.

(I have just questioned that last dark thought, wondering if I am being too dramatic. I still can't reconcile myself with sharing this stuff. It is much easier pretending to be fine, isn't it?)

During those difficult years, I slept every night with my left arm in a sling strapped around my waist and back in an effort to keep my arm in its socket. I would hope that when the fits came, they could not wrench my arm from me and steal hours, steal sleep, steal the likelihood of me fulfilling whatever I had boldly committed to do the next day.

I would have four or five fits a night. Sometimes they were quite small ones, fierce forces that tensed my muscles, pushed my limbs about, made me call out. Sometimes they were big ones lasting a couple of minutes, and making my body do the craziest things, like clamping my jaws down so hard they nicked strips off each side of my tongue, turning it black and blue for about a week.

Like thrashing so wildly that both arms were dislocated, leaving me to come around and have to work out who I was, where I was, before coming to the horrible realisation that I couldn't move my arms. Then there was the pain.

The pain.

I am no fan of childbirth. I believe, rightly, that it is the worst physical pain most women ever have to experience in their lives. It is, however, a pain that can be managed with gas and air. And you get a baby at the end of it, which is a bonus, depending on your view of newborns. Plus, people are nice to you, and bring you cute little outfits or flowers and say well done.

I can honestly say that having one's shoulders wrenched from their sockets is right up there above childbirth on my pain chart. When I was asked to rate this pain from one to ten, I always went for an eight because pain is relative and I was clearly not dead. Although being dead sometimes sounded like a cushy way out.

With dislocated shoulders there is no obvious end in sight. There is only pain, the inability to move because of the pain, and the massive dread of knowing you have to move to get into the ambulance and there will be a long wait between now and this pain being over, preceded by three men armed with pillow cases and straps coming to wrench the thing back in.

When help lies behind a locked front door at the bottom of a flight of stairs, you *can* get to it with a dislocated arm, mostly because you have to. Animal instinct kicks in and makes you unlock that door and twist the handle even though it's excruciating to do so. When help is on the other side of a door, you will get that door open.

My Lovely Mark would ring the ambulance, he would answer the twenty questions you need to answer to get a crew, and eventually they would come.

I can hear it now if I stop. The lovely rushing sound of an ambulance, racing down the road in the still of the early morning. No sirens, no one else around. Just a fast-moving thing and men with gas and air and morphine, salvation with flashing lights.

On those occasions that I didn't make it downstairs to the door myself, it was always weird when the ambulance crew double-act arrived in my bedroom in their jumpsuits, looking all capable and manly, whooshing in cold air and equipment.

And there was me, this weird, smelly, bleeding thing on the bed, gasping like a fish through the pain of my arm, dodgy pyjamas half on, the pain-sweat running down my arse crack, with breath that could melt plastic. And there they are, in my bedroom, where I was asleep just moments before, next to my husband.

They'd give me gas and air, try to get in a line for morphine, then get me down the stairs to the ambulance.

The morphine line did not usually go that well. Getting lines put into your foot really damn well hurts; on the pain scale I'd give it a four.

In truth, I have a problem with gas and air – or entonox, in the trade. I know I do. If I were ever to become a professional druggie, gas and air would be my drug of choice. I could easily do four canisters of the stuff between home and hospital. And it turns me into a complete arsehole. I become obsessed with people and their stories, start saying terrible things, talk twaddle and embarrass myself massively, like a drunk at a funeral.

I could not stand in front of the hundreds of ambulance crews who have rescued me over the years and ask them what I said. The shame would be too great.

I like to believe I was always polite, like to believe I was grateful. But I suspect I was a blathering mad woman covered in snot and tears, wearing tragic pyjamas and emanating the bad breath from hell.

I made a point of saying lots of nice things as soon as they arrived, pre-gas and air, in the hope they would remember me being grateful, not as the demented fitter ranting in the ambulance.

Inside A&E you can suck away on massive cylinders of gas and air as long as you keep yourself out of trouble and don't get so high you become a general nuisance. I used to imagine I was a free-diver, practising a particular sort of breathing – slow in, long out – so that over the hours waiting to be relocated I could keep myself balancing on the line between just conscious and completely off my face.

When the room starting spinning, or my speech slurred, or I thought I would be sick, I eased off for a bit.

The wait can be long with a dislocated arm, especially if

you are a regular. They know you can deal with it because you have before. And, given gas, air and a dark corner, you can get yourself to a place where you know you are not really an emergency case in its true sense.

I've been in the crash room on a trolley when half the world has come racing through, other patients in critical condition who seem a world away from me and my issues. I remember coming off a BA flight from Australia with a dislocated arm after I fell asleep on the flight, had a fit, put my arm out and had to sit like that for five hours until we landed. It was officially the worst flight ever.

They offered me a couple of paracetamol and made that announcement you never want to hear, asking whether there was a doctor on board. A paediatric specialist turned up, looked sorry for me, and left again. I kind of wished it had been a gynae specialist, just because there is humour in a master of the foof trying to relocate your buggered arm.

I even went to the onboard toilets with my arm dislocated. The weird folding door slammed behind me and I was stuck in there because I didn't have an arm free to get myself out. I had to cry for help from inside the cubicle. And no one wants to answer a cry for help from someone inside an airplane toilet.

I digress…

I ended up in A&E on New Year's Eve in some godforsaken hell hole near Heathrow.

No one wants to be in A&E on New Year's Eve, especially not one in the arse-end of London. I knew I was in trouble when I got there and the nurse looked like she'd dressed up as a nurse – and not a sexy one either – for a laugh. She had no clue what she was doing there and to this day is probably still staggering about the NHS picking up the shit shifts no one else wants to cover, with her rudimentary grasp of Romanian first-aid.

Those are desperate times, arriving in the place you need to help you – knowing full well that any consultant with a life and social skills will be absolutely off their face at a party. So you are left with the lunatics.

Having become something of a connoisseur of front-line medical professionals (and dodgy agency nurses who usually work at Lidl), I am an expert at sussing out whether or not someone is going to get my arm back in its socket, and how much pain will be involved.

Bear in mind I was still scared shitless, drunk on gas and air, and desperately in need of a wee at this point. And don't forget the crap hair and bad breath.

Bedside manner is everything.

You can tell if they are nervous about their own ability, a situation not improved by the fact that they think I am Katie Hopkins the Cowbag. One of the most depressing moments in A&E is discovering that the help you have available lacks the confidence – or the will – to actually help you.

I remember a young doctor coming to see me, sweating at the crotch, telling me he was going to try to get my arm back in. I looked at him. He looked apologetic. And we both smiled in unspoken acceptance: 'Never gonna happen.'

Sure enough, twelve hours later I was on a ward, arm still buggered, waiting for the surgeons to bang it back in under a general.

Others are cocky to the point of being ridiculous, and then you have the opposite problem. This type is usually dressed in a tight, red jumpsuit – the supermen of A&E.

I don't know what the red jumpsuits mean in official terms, but they suggest a history of lots of kinky sex at medical school, being brilliantly good at everything they touch, and having a legion of nubile girlfriends to pleasure in between shifts. All fuelled by unfettered access to the NHS drugs cupboard. I secretly applaud their derring-do.

These boys in red are as terrifying as the sweating new boy who is incapable of helping you. They don't just want to put your arm back in its socket; they want to prove their penis is unquestionably the biggest in the Primary Care Trust, or whatever administrative grouping is currently in vogue.

They want to test their skills, to wager with their mate that they can get it back in without knocking you unconscious to stop your banshee-wailing.

They tried to talk me into relaxing my arm and relaxing my shoulder, and reached for the hand on the end of my dislocated arm, oblivious of the fact that I was prepared to slaughter on sight anyone who came near it.

They stood there, holding onto the very thing that was crucifying my whole world, and told me to relax – all the while being handsome and dastardly self-assured while I sat there in my freaky pyjamas with spit and blood in my hair, and off my face on gas and air. I might've had a catheter hanging out of my foof, just for good measure.

And then they tried to manipulate the joint, taking me towards the crunch point where the bone should crack back into place, ratcheting up the pain, telling me to just relax, winking at the hot nurse who just flitted by.

When it wouldn't and I couldn't, and I finally made them give in and fetch the hard drugs, they dropped me like a stone.

I had failed to live up to the expectations set by their god-like A&E abilities. I had let them down with my whimpering and angry jawline. I had failed to let them prove that they are better than their mates. Perhaps their penises are not as big as they allege.

These episodes were always a tragically depressing experience.

I want to say to those people who have helped me at my most desperate: this isn't who I am. I am more than this. By day I am Katie Hopkins the fearless ball-breaker, even if, by night, I am this ugly, smelly thing having a wee on a com-mode in A&E, with my arse out and my arm out, unable to pull up my own pyjamas.

I have always struggled with the commode wee. I can be desperate to the point of imagining my belly will explode in a fountain of yellow and bits of bladder, but sit me on a commode in a room full of nurses, doctors and the odd po-liceman, or come face to face with my smelly bedtime foof as you pull down my sweaty pyjamas for me and nope, nothing. Not one drop.

I am sure I am not bothered by peeing in front of people. I've done it often enough, and I am desperate for the relief. But I am guessing my body and brain are more embarrassed than I am as a person, and so they won't perform.

And it's not like I am shy of how wee works, or about get-ting my bits out. I have had to wee in some truly desperate situations. Once, when I double-dislocated both arms in my sleep, I had to have a catheter inserted, in the unloading bay at St Thomas' Hospital. The nurse was so kind and I felt so bad about it. I cried rivers. I remember never having felt so reduced. No arms. A world of staff trying to work out how to fix me. And some poor woman fiddling with my urethra in the middle of the night so I didn't wet myself as well.

And yet, just hours before, I was Katie Hopkins, filming *If Katie Ruled the World* in front of a live studio audience, apparently invincible.

The Katie of that night is not a woman I want to think about or know. She is not a person, not living, just an animal existing. She is an injured thing after being run over, waiting at the vet for someone to put her out of her misery. I will not return to being her, no matter what.

Mum and Dad happened to witness that fit. They had come to stay for a night in the apartment I was in. They'd never seen this side of my life; I'd kept it my secret. Didn't want to worry them. The ambulance took close to three hours to get to me. And getting out of the apartment, with its narrow doors and tiny lifts, took another hour.

My dad said they would have put down an animal if it was suffering like that. He was right. I never understood why, sometimes, my body would not just give in and allow me to fall unconscious, just to give me a break, or to fall away completely and give up the whole fight. What was the point of a person whose brain was wired so badly?

In these hours, the most desperate hours, I just wanted the pain to go away, but in the hours after, the morning after, I wanted *everything* to go away. I used to imagine falling asleep and never waking up, how that wouldn't actually be too bad a thing – in fact, it might be quite nice to let them put me back together after I am gone and avoid the hard bit. I wanted to stop having to be brave and just let myself fall into the dark.

I still feel that way now, sometimes. I'm still at ease with death in that way. I can speak about dying easily and openly because I accepted it a long time ago. I write about death a fair bit too, and feel close to it. Sometimes I feel like I welcomed it into my life, at times wanted it to end my life, so now we can sit side by side, death and me, as if we are on the train together, chatting away about life as it passes by. I don't fear him.

Maybe that will change now I have been given this new, fit and free life. But I don't think so. The long sleep has always seemed to me to be a lovely thing at the end of a difficult life. With death by my side I am at ease when I think about it.

I also see the glamour of death. Of toddling off to sleep after putting a frozen chicken out on the side for the next day, only never to wake. Snatched from life when you weren't looking. I want to go like that – before I am old or mad or both.

In April 2015, surgeons at the National Hospital for Neurology and Neurosurgery said I had a life expectancy of under two years, that within the next two years, according to their experience and probability, I would have a big fit from which I would never regain consciousness or recover.

Mark sat with me for this news. It was delivered in a way that was professional and calm, but oddly menacing all the same.

I knew Professor Duncan was right. I knew there would be one big fit to end them all. Secretly, in the dark and in pain, in the margins of my life, I had already wished for it. It's a curious thing, to sit there with your professional and private life all in order – flourishing in some ways: a column in a national paper, a national radio show due to kick off, three healthy children, a loyal husband – and yet to be acutely conscious of the other you, the secret one, the sweating, crying, broken one with bits of brain still lost from the fits and memory still missing – this other you that would sometimes rather be dead.

A two-year window. Not two years in the way of a cancer patient. Not two years and maybe a bit longer if you are lucky, but within two years. Maybe tonight? Next week? One night when we are on holiday in Rhodes in the summer? Maybe in a hotel room on the road alone, lying there until my husband starts to worry why there is no text or call. A game of chance.

One night the Grim Reaper would come. But as a surprise. Without knocking.

Making friends with death seemed like a good idea, to understand his ways and to minimise the silence around him so that when he came we would all be just that little bit ready.

For my sanity, for my family's future, for some notion of hope, it also made sense to sign up for an operation that a team of surgeons was prepared to undertake.

My epilepsy was not in an easy spot. It was deep inside my head, parked up tight next to the part of my brain responsible for my sight. This was a massive operation that would either kill me or save me. Or save me, but leave me half dead.

I remember the head surgeon, Mr McEvoy, listing the risks. I remember every little thing about the room we were in: the light, the desk, the little notes scattered about, the kind faces of his team. And the word 'deficit'. The risk of deficit.

Risk of death.

Risk of loss of speech.

Risk of blindness.

Risk of loss of left hand.

Risk of loss of left hand and left leg.

Risk of change in personality.

Risk of change in who you are.

These things called 'deficits' were all potential further subtractions from the vague shell of sanity I was trying to preserve. If there had been a tick box, I would have gone for the death option.

The risks were of the sort I couldn't imagine dealing with, because the changes would be so massive. It made me think a lot about choice and coping.

If you are knocked down by a car or thrown from your horse and wake up in a hospital paralysed, you have no choice. Coping with partial paralysis after the event is obligatory. You cope. Or you kill yourself, which is another kind of choice.

But to make an active decision, to make a choice to be paralysed, is really odd. It's like being asked to give permission for the car to crash or the horse to ride you into a tree. You have to let the bad thing happen to you. You have to willingly agree to walk into the path of the car. To walk onto the labelled landmine. To cause yourself injury from which you might never recover.

I sometimes think the expression 'between a rock and a hard place' was invented for people like me. The rock was catastrophic epilepsy. And the hard place was the possible outcomes of a surgery that could save me. Knowing all the while that others have it worse. Others have it harder.

I say this honestly, without meaning to insult anyone. I do not mean to be cruel. But this is my truth: other patients that you see around the corridors of the National Hospital are like ghoulish reminders of what you might become. The hospital is a kind of zombie-land full of hideous monsters with bandaged heads, half skulls, dragging the left half of their body, trailing a leg behind them as they go, surrounded by sticks and helpers and dribble. Any one of them could be the future you. Is this really better, or is it worse? Is a short life better – or is a longer life half-lived worth more?

I used to dread my appointments in that place, a place of cures but also a place of horrors around every corner, reminders of what you might become. What would those people give to be normal, assuming they even knew what that was anymore?

And just two blocks away – a busy road, people driving without a care in the world. Jogging without thinking, their biggest drama being the fact that their phone is on 10 per cent charge.

Just like pain, worry is a relative thing. But that doesn't mean you would wish either on your enemies.

Just around the corner from the National Hospital, the walking hell of epileptic zombies and unfortunates with half heads (one of which I was to become), is Great Ormond Street Hospital for sick children.

Walking past this hospital is massive for me. When I was at my worst after surgery, missing the top of my head, meningitis blooming around my brain, throwing my left leg out awkwardly in front of me, with no sensation in my foot, I could still look at the children's hospital and know I was lucky.

I felt so sorry for the mums and dads inside waiting patiently by beds, hearts breaking because their children were hurting, wishing with all their might to be able to swap places with their babies and take the hurt for them.

I was lucky my own children were still sleeping around the corner in an apartment we rented, tucked up safe with their dad. Mostly healthy and doing OK at this thing called life. Poppy able to walk. India seeing the world sort of brilliantly at an angle of 90 degrees. Perfect-pants Max crashing through, untroubled. I sense that my expectations as a mother are set according to very different parameters from those of my pushy-parent friends.

Whatever happens, my children are well, and whatever happens, I haven't given them my epilepsy. Mine is not genetic. I have not cursed my children. I will not plague their lives.

When I get an email from a mum or grandma talking about their child or grandchild with epilepsy, my heart sinks. Knowing what I know. Knowing what my husband has seen with me. Knowing his face when it takes longer than normal for life to come back behind my open eyes. Knowing that at times I welcomed death as an option.

I can only begin to imagine being a parent watching their child suffering through all that, but I cannot go far with the thought. I have no answers, I daren't look too closely. I can only admire their bravery and pretend to be brave me and show them what is possible.

There is much that is weird about marrying a night-time epileptic, but somehow my husband has not been defeated by any of it. Not the massive fits, or the arm dislocations, or the months when my fits made me angry and unreasonable. Fits that made me believe nonsense and create huge arguments out of nothing, storming out of the house while my brain scrambled everything I thought I knew.

The only thing that terrified the poor sod was the 'eyes open but no one home' thing.

After a big fit, I would be left wide-eyed, staring, but vacant. Mark would get me through the bone crunching, hold my arms through the fit, watch my head for sharp corners, and mind my tongue afterwards, but he hated the bit that followed: waiting for the person to come back behind the eyes.

I would lie there, open eyes rolled back in my head, with nothing behind them. Simply nothing. I was just a broken bleeding thing, not a person, and Mark was all alone in the dark, in this big old house with our three children and this blank-eyed thing that was not me.

I have ten GCSEs, four A-levels and an Economics degree; I am a working mum. And yet, after a fit, you could ask me what day it is or the date of my birthday or where we are right now, and I couldn't have told you.

Knowing you don't know the answers is one of the most terrifying things.

I can still feel the tears, looking back at ambulance crews and crying, not just because I didn't know, but because of what that meant: that I had no memory, that my whole world was falling away to the point that I didn't know my own birthday.

I wonder if that is what dementia feels like. Knowing you don't know things you should, not being able to retrieve the most basic information, knowing your brain is battered, addled.

I wonder now how far the line is between me and dementia. I wonder how long I have got. Dementia is very present in my life, like death; there is no hiding from the truth that my brain has been pummelled into semi-consciousness twice or three times a week over a long period of time.

I wonder when I find myself putting washing in the fridge. Or the coffee away in the washing machine, or the hot water bottle away in the microwave.

When I get lost finding my way out of a hotel, or can't believe I have ever seen a film before, I wonder.

Is this me? Is it starting?

Fits destroy your brain. They damage it with the shaking. Like a boxer pounded in the head, or a rugby player knocked sideways.

We shall just have to wait and see.

I try to prepare my children now. Tell them that when I don't know who they are, they are not to bother visiting me any more. Tell them to bash me on the head if I don't know where I am. Tell them if I don't know where I am I no longer want to be there.

I want to relieve them of any duty of care now, and take my guilt with me.

This is what's behind my preoccupation with euthanasia. The reason I want to get hold of the little pill you can get to keep in your cupboard so that when your time comes you can choose to sleep instead, to fall into the night.

I have met with Dr Nitschke, or 'Doctor Death' as he calls himself. He helped patients to die when euthanasia was, for a brief period, legal in Australia. He still considers it his mission to provide ways for people to end their lives gracefully and free of pain. I support him absolutely.

I met him during the filming of my chat show, *If Katie Hopkins Ruled the World*. I wanted to understand why he believed so strongly in the right to die when you choose. I even tried his machine, which you attach yourself to, answer questions confirming your decision to end your life, then self-administer a lethal dose of gas to do the job.

It was a sobering moment.

But it's his pill I want – a little white pill. It's still available from Asia and South America, but an offence to have in your possession.

I think everyone should have the option of having one of these in their bathroom cupboard. Not to take. Not to rush you to the end of life. And not because you aren't wanted by the world. But for the comfort of knowing it is there. If life is a gift, then surely it is also ours to give back?

I actually think a euthanasia pill like this would prolong my life. It would allow me to keep going, knowing I could control the end when I was ready and still continent. That I would not have to jump early because eventually there would be no one there to push.

These may sound like dark thoughts but I think they are just practicalities, the conversations you need to have with

yourself when you have to face up to big things. I don't sub-
scribe to the idea of not talking about things because they are
too awful. Talk about it and perhaps it may seem a little less
awful some of the time.

It was a brain tumour that gave me four fits a night and
seizures powerful enough to throw my shoulders from their
sockets forty-three times in twelve months, and it's over
a year now since I had brain surgery to fix the problem. 'A
right parietal resection for a focal cortical dysplasia', if you
must know. There were never any guarantees with the surgery. No guarantees I would make it through, or make it back
as me.

There were just percentages. Percentage of not making it
back? Less than ten. Percentage of making it back with some
damage to the left arm and left leg? Much higher.

Percentage of being changed? Certain.

I remember the brilliant psychologist at the hospital test-
ing me before surgery and telling me: 'Loss of brain function
is the door price you pay to roll the dice at the casino of neurosurgery.' It is possibly one of my favourite quotes of all time,
purely because of the overwhelming fear it inspires.

Just two months before my operation I was honest with
her that I still didn't know if I could go through with it. I was
terrified, sweating at even the thought of it, still lacking courage – not so much about not coming back at all, but about
coming back damaged. Or coming back as only some fraction
of myself, or even with some other person in my body.

I am not unique. Just yesterday I had a message from a lady
whose brain surgery to remove a tumour was just two days

away. 'Not feeling very brave,' she wrote. She was planning to work right up until the last minute.

But I've learned. Before having surgery that could take your life, you don't need to be brave. And you don't need to have courage or pretend it's OK.

It's fine to say you are scared. To say you are terrified, even. Your only job is to hold on, by your fingertips if necessary. To hang on and keep sane until you get on that trolley and the cold rushes up your arm.

I wasn't even brave enough to tell my three children, who were eleven, ten and seven at the time.

Despite all my lectures to them: 'If you have a problem, you tell mummy. And mummy will help you fix it.' Despite always promising to be honest with them. Despite imagining how they would feel if I popped off and never even said goodbye.

I just couldn't fill their little heads up with worry. We mums want to seem invincible to our kids. I'd always told mine I would be there for them, I would never leave them.

What if they looked back and realised I had lied?

In the weeks before the surgery, I changed. I started cuddling them at night and telling them a slightly different message: 'I'll always be here for you, no matter what. And even when, one day, I pop off, I'll still be watching, wishing you to be safe. Even if you can't see me, I'll be just next door. Listening.'

I was trying to get them to keep talking to me, even if I never came back. I'm not sure if it was for me or them, that impulse to stay part of their brilliant lives even if I was gone.

I didn't have the emotional courage to say goodbye to my

own mum. We are the same two people. We share the same naughty gene, and a soft one, too. If I want sensible advice, I ask my dad. If I want someone to agree I should do something I know I shouldn't, I ask my mum.

We agreed when she came to my house to take over the children and our world for a bit, we wouldn't even try to talk. Wouldn't even acknowledge what we might be needing to say. We would pass each other outside the garage, and the children wouldn't see us get upset.

And we did.

As I left, still terrified, I wondered if that would be the last time I got to smell my children's hair. Or see my mum.

In advance, to help me hang on, I made plans. What I couldn't face emotionally, I handled practically with Mark. We met financial advisers and put money into accounts for the children and Mark to access without me.

We centralised any savings or pensions under Mark's name.

I made a folder of doom with all the paperwork Mark might need: birth certificates, wedding certificates, divorce statement, dull bits of paper – the stuff that helps sort out a life after death.

And I organised ahead. I sent mum her Mother's Day and birthday cards, writing all the things I couldn't bring myself to say out loud. I made sure I said thank you to everyone who has helped me in life. I popped my head in here and there, not mentioning the operation but making sure I had signed off with a smile.

It's a curious thing, tidying up your life in case it might be over. But sometimes the act of coping amounts to nothing more than getting things done. Even if my children hated me for leaving, they would see I'd tried my best to make sure they had everything they needed when I was gone.

Looking back, I would do all this again. When things seem very dark, knowing you left things tidy feels nice. Like the way we like to get the ironing done and the kitchen cleaned before a holiday, so we can come back to a nice house. Only this time, I wasn't sure I was coming back.

I slept on the ward the night before my operation, with my husband in a hotel round the corner. It felt better being there; the leaving, the big dread, was over.

In the morning I felt calmer than I'd felt for months. No more trying to be brave, no more pretending to the children that I was tough. I didn't even have to hang on now. I just listened to the doctors, the anaesthetists, the surgeons. Listened, nodded, said thank you.

I sat there calmly, having disinfected myself in the shower, with support tights rolled high, my neck marked to show it was my right side that needed the knife and my hair waiting to be shaved.

I wondered if this same calm comes over people preparing for death – the strange wash of inevitability that makes you fearless because you are suddenly powerless.

I suspect it's the same for all of us who have faced life-threatening surgeries, diseases, tumours or cancers, who have diced with death, chanced it all in the hope of a better life.

I was supposed to be in surgery for eight hours. Twelve hours and thirty minutes later I was out and in intensive care. It struck me, as I looked up at my husband, that he'd suffered more than I had.

I must admit that it's been hard, and the journey to recovery has felt long.

Post-surgery bacterial meningitis didn't help. I had to have my skull reopened twice more, and eventually the flap of bone protecting my brain was removed to stop the infection squashing the life out of me.

I have felt like a freak, and endured people's sympathetic stares. My brain no longer speaks to my left leg like it did before, and I have had to relearn the art of climbing stairs. When I'm anxious, I can't remember anything I just said.

When I went back to the psychologist six months after the surgery to test how much function I had lost, I cried before I even started the test, knowing she was about to expose how stupid I had become. My shame was absolute. There was no hiding now. No pretending I was OK.

She told me this is typical of people like me who are determined to be able to do stuff and are humiliated by limitation. But despite some tears, I have learned a few things about life after surgery, things I share with hundreds of men and women who have trodden the same path in different ways.

First: architects are arseholes.

Stairs that curve, are uneven, are at an angle or have no handrail are all a curse.

To you, these details are about aesthetics. To me, they initiate a complete collapse of confidence; once, in KFC, they made me break down and weep because I couldn't use them and I felt like a moron.

I will never tut at an old person moving slowly on stairs

ever again. If anything, I will carry their bag and hold their hand.

Second: having hair matters.

I pretended I was bigger than my hair, better than vanity. Me? Katie Hopkins? I don't need hair!

But I do.

Having no hair is really chilly. Bald men are actually hard as nails.

The sympathetic looks I received for having tufts of hair were hard to take. People thought I was dying of cancer (as, indeed, many bald people are). It's awkward.

Never tell a bald woman that you can get really realistic wigs these days. It might be true, but you can get really realistic strap-on penises too, and that doesn't mean all women want one. What we actually want is our hair back. What we don't need is more humiliation when our wig gets blown off by a Dyson Airblade hand dryer.

Third: don't pretend to be OK.

Even if you have spent twenty-five years pretending you are 'doing great', don't do it in hospital just so you can get home. I pretended I was feeling better to get home, when actually spinal fluid was leaking from my head, and I ended up with bacterial meningitis. Doctors don't need you to be brave. They need you to be polite but honest.

Fourth: never go shopping on morphine.

I did. This top was the result. I rest my case.

Fifth: don't make your pain the benchmark.

When people want to moan to you about their toothache,

don't give them the face that says: 'I survived brain surgery and meningitis.' Look like you care, make ouch faces, and offer them drugs. Don't play Top Trumps with suffering, even when you'd win hands down.

Sixth: don't settle for survivor.

There comes a point, a few months after surgery, when you become proud that you survived, that you can dress yourself and don't have to pee through a tube or in a shower sitting down. Do not let this be your new standard.

My young radio producer looked at me one day (no makeup/mud-coloured hair) and said, 'Will you stop being such an f*cking cancer patient and step up.' She had a point. I came back the following week with pink hair and makeup. And I felt like a new woman.

And finally: tiptoeing the high wire of life will make you a better person.

You will love your family more deeply, respect your husband for the things he saw and cleaned up, and have a new perspective on what really matters. You will still get angry when no one changes the toilet roll, but you will love your life because you got a second chance. And you can't buy those at John Lewis.

DEAR CHILDREN

Dear children,

You are safe at school now. I like walking you there because I get to hear more about what you are thinking and there is space for me to listen.

And I understand more about how you see the world at ten, nine and six. It is not exactly insightful stuff – 'Why the hell would you buy a car the same colour as your kid's hair?' – but if these are your biggest worries, I am serving you well.

I won't always be here to do that. You know that Mum's doctor says her epilepsy will get her one day. Fruit loops say karma will. But either way, I wanted to write down a few things for you to remember as you get bigger.

- *Never trust a zebra crossing. Just because they are named after a friendly animal doesn't mean drivers accord them the respect they deserve. The one near your school is lethal. Think Guardian, Daily Mail and The Independent: left, right and no one cares.*
- *Girls are weird. If the girls in your class start to make you feel upset about yourself, find some boys to hang out with. Girls think handbags matter. This is one step away from being a Scientologist.*

- *Sometimes doing well is reason enough for other people to put you down. If someone frowns at you, smile back. Absorbing ill will makes you stronger. And I want you to be the strongest person you can be.*
- *When you get older and kiss boys or girls or both, you will wonder why some people seem so amazing. Remember, everyone has to wee. Weeing makes us all the same, no matter how fantastic someone looks in a dress.*
- *We agree, Tampax make great mice. But not everyone thinks like us. Sometimes we are odd. This is OK too.*
- *One day you might think you want to stay with one person for the rest of your life. Perhaps you will want to wear a big white dress to celebrate. Ask yourself: 'Will I look back in five years and think I looked a right twat?' Mummy wishes she had done this.*
- *I hope to be there for your big day but, more importantly, I want to be there if it all goes wrong. My mum was there for me when this happened. You girls were a year old and less than a month old back then. And your grandma and grandpa somehow made it all OK.*
- *Most of all, I want you to find the fun like we do – to dance in your kitchen, wear pants on your head because leg holes make great eye holes and eat chips in the rain.*

If you forget all this, that's OK. Mummy made some royal cock-ups that are well documented on Google, but has no regrets and wouldn't change a single thing. Especially not the three of you.

Wherever I am, I will always be in the room just next door.

Love you lots

Mum

CHAPTER 5

POLITICS AND RELIGION

Politics and religion: the two things they say you should never talk about in polite company. I'd throw anal sex in there as a third, but I'm not sure it makes the list of things that average middle-class people tend to talk about over a Sunday roast anyway.

Like most things in life, I am pretty clear about my politics and my religion, and thought it might be helpful to lay them out here in this chapter so you can see how much we agree or disagree.

Maybe you could give yourself a score from 1 to 5 based on how strongly you agree, and we could do a little summary at the end, like they have in the magazines, where I tell you what your score says about you.

Buzzfeed, Vice and others do this sort of stuff quite regularly online. 'How Katie Hopkins are you?' they ask, and then present you with a quote. Who said this: Katie Hopkins or Hitler? Katie Hopkins or some other maniacal figure from history?

And they do have a point. Some of my sayings repeated out loud and out of context in the cold light of rush hour can sound a bit mad. But if we want to put a positive and somewhat narcissistic spin on things (as we should do in today's self-obsessed society), then what we can pull out from this is that at least people are hearing what I say. And some of the most evil monsters in history were also pretty damn iconic, depending on your perspective or your religion.

I am heartily encouraged that so many of my loyal follower base can score 100 per cent on those quizzes because they know how I talk and have learned some of my more important quotes off by heart.

You might imagine this is my ego speaking. That I am so full of self-love I want people to be able to quote Katie Hopkins in the street, right into the faces of liberals. And you might not be wrong.

But I see these mantras as helping to equip an entire generation with the force and tenacity to stand strong against the torrent of leftie nonsense they are obliged to withstand on an almost daily basis.

When you bump into some vegan lunatic in grunge wear, stocking up on a monthly supply of quinoa and laxatives at their health food store, a little voice in your head might shout: 'Animals stay alive for a reason. If we don't eat cows, cows won't exist. Your teeth have evolved for red meat. Your brain has dissolved for quinoa.'

When someone is playing a massive victim card and instructing you that you have violated their rights as a transracial pescatarian, the Hopkins voice in your head will say: 'I do not give offence. You choose to take it. You need to make better decisions.'

If someone asks: 'What is the point of you? Why do you even exist?' then you will be right there, ready with this: 'People like you, who have tried to silence people like me, have given me a voice. You are Doctor Frankenstein. And I am your monster.'

Or if some militant midwife is forcing you to latch your baby on to your bleeding nipples when neither it nor you can be arsed and you are still in a state of shock because something the size of a watermelon just exited your polo-mint-sized hole, you might remember: 'Breast is not best. It just rhymes. So do paedo and Speedo and neither of these things is OK.'

And if you are a mother, when a supermother at the school gate in charge of bake sales and voluntary after-school baking classes tries to strong-arm you into volunteering, maybe the little devil Hopkins will sit on your shoulder and help you explain how you see parenting, in the hope she will go away and interfere with someone else: 'I think of children like dogs. Always hungry, needing to run wild at least twice a day, and trained to shit in the right place.'

Or if a teacher tried to instil in you that all Brexit voters are knuckle-dragging Neanderthals and Trump equals hate, on the basis that he want to build a wall, then you have this goodie ready to go:

Opinions cannot be right or wrong. Life is not an exam and you are not an invigilator.

Once you have these little expressions locked and loaded, you will always have an answer. Or, at least, a little voice in your head telling you it is OK to think differently than the blithering idiot in front of you who equates their opinion with their sense of self. At the very least you'll be able to respond with a wry smile when you are surrounded by tossers busily agreeing with each other somewhere in Shoreditch over wheat beers and calamari.

So here we go. Here is a curated selection of my views on politics and religion. You get to rate how strongly you disagree. Or, indeed, agree. But perhaps I can ask one thing of you: that when you read my views – no matter how strongly you believe I am wrong – remember they are being said by the same woman I have showed you thus far. The same hopeless mum, the same idiot wife, the same me. Just me. Not a panto monster.

Some of you will agree but feel guilty about it. Or feel the need to shower. You lot are the sort that tweet 'I hate Katie Hopkins, but...' whenever you agree with something I say, signalling to your leftie chums and liberal mates that you are still safe.

You're so frightened about your mates disowning you for agreeing with something I say, you feel obliged to express how much you hate me. I think that says an awful lot more about you and your level of self-confidence than it does about me. I do notice you, stalking my Twitter feed rather than outing yourself and following it. Just in case one of your mates spots you following me and has a go at you for it. You are virtually an opinion handmaid from *The Handmaid's Tale*, fellating your friendship circle, obeying group-think, pandering for their affection, hoping they will keep wanting to shove their opinions up your arse.

When I was fired (sorry, 'agreed to leave') my radio show for a poorly written tweet, I received texts like this:

'We may not have agreed on everything, but I admire your courage. And thought you were great on the radio.'

Lesson: don't preface. We don't need to agree for *me* to be an OK person. *You* are the one who is struggling with the idea of how you can like someone but not agree with them.

If you strongly agree with everything I say, and feel no sense of shame, you are quite possibly already a loyal member of the Hopkins army and I thank you. Or perhaps you even enjoy the idea that we should all have the space and freedom to stand up for what we believe (as long as it is legal) without being physically assaulted in the street.

I have digressed. Here we go:

ISRAEL V PALESTINE

I love Israel, even though I have never been there. I love Benjamin Netanyahu, and his ex-spokesperson, Mark Regev, is a man I want to meet and marry. He is pencilled in as husband number five. Mark Regev's ability to defend his Prime Minister and deflect criticism and skewed reporting from the left-wing press was nothing short of miraculous. How Trump has not seconded him to the White House to take charge there is beyond me.

Israel is a country that is ostensibly governed by those who see things in black and white, which appeals to my inner pragmatist. There are not too many grey areas in Israel. Except the land border with Palestine, perhaps, and, indeed, Palestine's right to land. But we'll slide over this sticky subject as no good will come of it and, whichever way you dress, you have undoubtedly already made up your mind on that one.

Benjamin Netanyahu appears to have my outlook on life: either you wish our country well, or you wish our country harm. And you need to decide in which camp you sit.

If you wish our country well, we will look after you and your family and protect you with everything we have. We will support you, pay you well and make sure you are as healthy as you can be.

If you wish our country and the people in it harm, then stand by. If you launch a rocket at our country, we will obliterate you. We will warn you first. We might even give you a call to tell you to get out of the way. And then we will destroy your home and the homes of your family and your pets.

By implication, if your son is a twat, you are a twat, and if you die in the crossfire, it is his fault and you only have him to blame.

They take the same approach to stabbings. If you come into a temple and stab Israeli soldiers, Israel will shut your temple. No matter how religious you are or how much you need to chat to whatever god you happen to follow; you will have to do that somewhere else. A public toilet perhaps.

And if you think you can stab one of our officers and get away with it – you can't. We will gun you down in a heartbeat. And then evict your family from their homes too, for being disloyal. And gun down anyone else near you who happens to be carrying a knife.

Israel has got it bang on the money. And the fact that our left-wing university campuses cannot stand Israel and are wildly pro-Hamas makes me love Israel even more. The fact that our idiot London mayor allows pro-Hamas marchers to parade through London waving the Hezbollah flag reinforces my commitment to Bibi. The fact that Corbyn and the left refuse to condemn the terrorism of Hamas is all I need to know: I am on the side of the good and the great. And the rest are wrong.

If you are ever bored and feel like watching the softest of soft porn in a public place, or are in need of a pretend boy-friend, sign up to the Twitter account of the Israeli Defence Force.

I have.

It is like bathing in testosterone. Like a soothing balm, to be applied liberally all over your body when you feel like a dried up old spinster surrounded by men who are more proud of their hipster beards than their low-hanging balls.

When I die I want to make a substantial donation to the IDF beer fund, so they can toast the death of a good friend.

UKIP

People always assume I am a Kipper (UKIP supporter), mainly because I was the lone Brexit voice in London for the duration of the referendum campaign and had Leave signs up in my garden until the night of 23 June. Each time one was stolen by some irritating leftie, I put another one back in its place.

I read about a gentleman in the United States who was so sick of Democrats stealing his signs in support of Trump and the Republicans, he managed to wire his sign up to the mains; the thief got 120 volts coursing through his veins mid-robbery and was nearly killed.

Naturally the homeowner got off with no charge, because America is awesome.

No matter how stony the road and how wonky the path we take, no matter how many times Remainers try to derail the process, and when, finally, Brexit is quashed by the anti-democratic establishment, I will always be emotionally buoyed by the certain knowledge Leave won, and I knew they would because I listened. And I was alive in a time when the rest of the UK (i.e. not London) had their voices heard.

Watching the results come in on a huge screen (I happened to be on a massive yacht in Cannes for my work, prostituting my goodwill for Mail Online) will always be one of the highlights of my time in this job of mine. I went to bed at 6 a.m., giddy with the thrill of it all. I could have kissed every Englishman that voted.

Sometimes we forget that we are fortunate to live in these times. Living through Brexit more than compensated for not being around at the time of JFK, who was a hottie. It's probably not as great as living in Churchillian England, but it has to be said the war probably was a bit of a pain in the arse, and I am told Churchill was actually very overweight, quite short and unfit, so the folklore about him may well be very much better than the truth, and his posthumous life, encapsulated in the recordings of his radio speeches, may well represent his finest hours.

Anyway, I am not a Kipper and have never voted UKIP. Splitting the vote was never going to help the Tory Party succeed. It does not pay to vote with your heart, only with your head.

I would assert that UKIP was never a real party. I am not diminishing it – quite the opposite: its strength lay in the authenticity of its support base, which was made up of well-meaning patriots who wanted the best for their country and were proud to call themselves British. And my heart goes out to each and every one of them who had been forced to watch politicians destroy the opportunity they voted for and dreamed of: a sovereign British nation.

NIGEL FARAGE

My biggest criticism of UKIP – which is a direct criticism of Nigel Farage – is his singular failure to plan for his succession and, worse than that, the way he actively conspired against strong potential candidates who would have taken the party forward.

Suzanne Evans was a victim in this. I met her at a UKIP conference where she had been shoved into a backroom and blacklisted from appearing on the stage. Farage recognised the real contenders for his crown and got rid of them as fast as he could.

He operated like a vortex, sucking everything in towards him, enjoying the power but failing to dissipate it or devolve it through the ranks. It is a criticism I would level at him directly if he ever showed any curiosity about what the people around him thought.

When Farage stepped down and the Conservatives took on the UKIP manifesto and gave us a referendum, then promised a hard Brexit, UKIP's job was done.

I maintain that UKIP made momentous change happen, and gave a great deal of pleasure and belief to the very many who are disillusioned by globalists and their relentless propaganda about multiculturalism being a good thing. And Farage should be rewarded for this. Some call for him to be knighted. While I support their calls, I don't believe in the House of Lords, so I think maybe a little trophy and a certificate would be better. A mug, perhaps.

Farage is a serial schmoozer and as sharp-elbowed as the best of them. Watching him swan about the Lords like... well, Lord Muck, would be annoying. I suspect the House of Lords is much like an old people's home, with waterproof carpet tiles and a lingering and gag-inducing smell of talcum powder, Estée Lauder's 'violet' scent and old wee.

Farage failed to deliver on his EU referendum because, knowing he was about to walk away, he needed to have someone strong in place to hand the UKIP baton to in order to drive it over the line. Or if he wasn't prepared to hand over the limelight (he wasn't) then he needed to keep going and get Brexit over the finish line himself. But he didn't.

Handing the baton over to Paul Nuttall (in an election so duplicitous, candidates walked away to avoid validating the process) was the equivalent of me handing over a boiling pan of water to a three-year-old. Things were bound to go tits up and someone would get burned.

They did. 17.4 million people, in fact. Farage failed to plan for a successor, so he planned to fail.

Which is all very well for him. He is still milking the Farage fan club and his media career.

I have met Farage. And I don't *want* to say the experience was disappointing but… the experience was disappointing.

The idea of Nigel is way better than the reality of Nigel. He is far better as an idea of a person standing up for Britain with really good soundbites than he is in real life.

He is always accompanied by some terribly disappointing small boy (usually a chubster with a posh accent who is a bit too cocksure). His last assistant was arrested off the tarmac at Chicago airport after being caught in an FBI cash laundering sting.

My take is that he is as much a master of the political game as those he criticises. When all is said and done he's still a trader turned politician wearing the costume of the working man in the street.

There are parallels I believe with my security uniform at Disneyland Paris. Costumes can be deceiving.

That said, I'd still give him a certificate and a badge for pushing Cameron into a referendum and for making 17.4 million people feel very proud. However temporarily.

THE SILENCED MASSIVE

What is interesting, given that the Tory Party is in a mess, the Labour Party is feeling pretty perky and UKIP has died a dramatic death, is that vast swathes of people across the UK are left not served by a party, and without a voice in the media.

It is the reason people like me continue to have a voice.

This is a point that bears repeating: between 15 and 20 million people in the UK, are currently unrepresented by a political party or by a media outlet that reflects their political position.

Because of the thought monopoly of London, and the media monopoly that gives voice to the capital's thoughts, a quarter of the country feels their voices are not heard. Over a quarter of the country. Imagine that. And imagine how much government interference must have gone on to make that possible.

And on that point, I present to you...

THE BBC

Now I know I should be grateful to the BBC. They let me on their little show *The Apprentice* back in the day when it was actually quite good and not a random combo of two wildly different formats (*The Apprentice* and *Dragon's Den*).

I was on the third series of the show, I think. After the Badger (Ruth Badger, the 2006 runner-up in the second series) and before it became ridiculous. Like all the other muppets, I competed in a number of tasks and was one of the handful who managed to survive till the end without killing someone else, or themselves, or being removed for being duller than *Newsnight*.

By the time I got to the final, I had realised that I wasn't prepared to spend six months pissing about in Brentwood working at Sir Alan's computer factory while TV land caught up with the real world. So I told him to stick the job.

Not only that, of course, but given my daughter was about to go and have her hip broken and rebuilt and be stuck in a human plaster cast for three months, my loyalties lay firmly elsewhere, certainly not on a pretend set, in the quest for a phantom job created to please fickle viewers of telly.

But the point rather remains that without my foray into *The Apprentice* I wouldn't be here now writing this, wouldn't have been a columnist in national papers, wouldn't have had the opportunities to have a voice and a platform.

But that's pretty much where my gratitude to the BBC ends.

Without government intervention it would not be possible for such an inefficient and sprawling bureaucracy with such heavy political bias to exist. It simply could not happen. In the free market, facing real competition, the BBC would not and could not survive.

To counter the fact that no one would be prepared to willingly support twenty layers of management, endless HR meddling, and diversity-mafia tactics that distort any notion of equitable treatment, regular taxpayers are forced to fund it all. Every single last idiotic bit of it.

Because the BBC could not be supported by the truth of the free market, it is funded by us. A compulsory taxation, channelled directly into the pockets of those whose mouthpiece it is, and who are controlled by direct links to the power and money of the establishment.

This is never a good thing. What is even stranger is that in an age of multi-platform digital content and relentless demand for immediacy and demand-led programming, we have this old centrist monolith that demands we keep paying for it. Roughly 90 per cent of what I see on screen is entirely at odds with the way I think.

The BBC is able to apply nonsense diversity criteria to everything first, before any consideration of its purpose and its role, to the extent that you have to employ a black guy from a sink estate brought up exclusively on free school meals before you are even allowed to consider what programme you might be making.

Here's one example. A Muslim rape squad has just been sentenced in Newcastle. Full plaudits to the police force there for doing a fabulous job.

BBC *Newsnight* had a discussion on Muslim grooming gangs and why the problem seems to be so widespread. Five people were invited on to the show to discuss the issue.

And all five were Muslims. Specifically of the view that Muslim rape gangs have nothing to do with being a Muslim because men who rape young white girls use alcohol and drugs, and good Muslims don't do that sort of thing.

It's enough for me to take the telly and chuck it at the wall in my lounge.

Absolutely have someone on to defend the Islamic faith. But why not have the police chief heading up the investigation, too? Or someone from the community sick of these gangs being labelled Asian? Or better still, some of the victims and survivors? Or some of the ladies whom I have met and spoken to who were abused? Where are their voices?

I still pay my BBC TV licence because breaking the law and being harassed for it is not my thing. And I would be made an example of.

But I disagree with it vehemently. And if I were not marginally in the public eye I can't honestly say I would pay it. I cannot condone a regressive tax on the poor that ends up in the hands of London types earning over a million a year. Nothing about that is fair.

And the fact the output is so biased – laundering news to make it palatable to the left, as per the example above – makes this a broadcaster of pure propaganda.

Even for a regular BBC contributor, as I am, there is bias at work. Contributors are assessed for their ethnic, sexual or social diversity before their opinion. And from the inside, the inefficiency is everywhere you look. As is the BBC's partisan nature.

When I was called in as part of a planned documentary on Trump, the proposed director for our piece said management had called him in and asked – while cowering behind their hands (like children) – whether he would be prepared to work with me. Like I was some kind of scary monster.

I find this kind of anecdote to be the most revealing of all. Grown adults who are senior managers at the BBC with colossal salaries and pension plans, asking if someone will work with you, hiding their faces behind their hands. Could this really be our non-partisan BBC at work, bastion of all that is balanced and without bias?

As we saw in Chapter 2, when I was asked to contribute to *The Media Show* for Radio 4 – for which they do not pay a fee – I was informed they would not even pay my travel expenses to get to the studio (a two-hour train journey for me). I reminded them that *they* had called to invite *me* onto the show. Contributors like me are expected to give up their time for free. Yet the production staff use the budget as a tool to try to prevent you from getting on air.

If a junior maker of the production team does not want you on, they will contrive to make it so you reject the invitation. Two can play at that game of course.

The other day an executive producer asked me to take a confirmed booking in my diary and make it a heavy pencil. As in,
not pencilled in, and not penned in, but heavy pencilled in.
Like an interim stage between being on or off, with the onus on
me to be hopeful. These are the mercenary egomaniacs you are
expected to deal with if you want the privilege of contributing
to the BBC at your own expense. Egomaniacs being paid salary,
expenses and pension at the same time as reminding you they
do not pay contributors a fee and expecting you to waggle your
tail like a happy puppy dog and be grateful to be patted.

You have to be very committed to your views and willing
to make a principled stand at your own expense if you want
to be part of the national conversation.

Then there are the myriad other dissenters and naysayers,
from TV commissioners to presenters, to newspaper owners
and well-connected establishment figures who turn the echo
chamber into one vast liberal hell hole, agreeing the news at
the weekend in Chipping Norton, and feeding it to the 'plebs'
like me in the week.

And despite spending £1.05 billion on the refurbishment of
Old Broadcasting House and the addition of New Broadcasting House, running an incredible £100 million over budget,
it is still a rabbit warren of damp toilet-cubicle-sized studios
with broken headsets and miserable looking interns.

Even in New Broadcasting House things don't work. Furni-
ture that was never designed for actually sitting on never gets
sat on. The real work happens in hard-to-find, out-of-the-way
places, while the main areas are given over to empty space
with jazzy carpets and meaningless signage.

The TV show mocking the BBC – *W1A* – did not have to work very hard for material. And is seen as hilarious by those happily taking a stonking salary and pension from this holy hell of ineptitude, funded by the taxpayer. It's a funny show. But I think the joke is very much on us.

We are laughing at a show mocking how much money is wasted by incompetents. But when you realise we are paying for all of it, it's not so damn funny.

At Radio 5, for example, a studio in constant use with a host of guests and presenters, the green room is the corridor. No one ever actually thought about how this space might be required to work, and it shows. It is the ultimate horse designed by committee, and an establishment monkey making the final decisions, leaving you with a camel and bananas for security.

Madness, chaos, inefficiencies and overwhelming partisanship; it is not a place of which I am fond. I have many informers on the inside desperate to get out, too.

It tends to be that the bigger the arsehole, the more they get paid and the higher up the chain of authority they rise – at which point they usually do something so monumentally stupid even they have to leave, so another aspiring arsehole can have an opportunity to shine his fat, white arse at the people paying his wages.

Pocket-sized crazy man Danny Cohen is a classic case in point. Having reached the top of the tree with a militant left-wing streak that would have made him an outstanding leader for Jeremy Corbyn's Momentum network, Cohen decided the most sensible thing he could do in the office was fire Jeremy

Clarkson, the BBC's biggest star and presenter of its most commercially lucrative show, *Top Gear*.

Flouncing about like a dwarf Schnauzer on acid, Cohen single-handedly culled the only BBC programme I was happy paying for and which presented me with any kind of return on my considerable investment.

I was not alone in my outrage. This was another classic case of London versus the rest of the UK. A liberal idiot, deafened by diversity quota and globalist nonsense, unable to hear the roars of laughter from the rest of the UK for a programme they loved.

A million supporters of Clarkson signed a petition to try to keep his *Top Gear* on the road, which was driven to the BBC HQ (feral husk of a building) in a tank.

But Cohen was determined. He had wanted Clarkson out for as long as he could remember, and was not going to miss the opportunity to claim a right-wing scalp.

This is what happens when you separate a company from the need to generate cashflow. And what happens when some of your biggest talent is not handled correctly because your militant political bias makes you think they are an utter git and therefore deserve to be treated like one.

TURKEY

I have long been suspicious of Turkey. Not only because it blackmailed the EU for cash handouts in return for promises to try to keep Syrian migrants in Turkey – instead of shoving them up the arse end of Greece – but because the guy running the place is a complete nutter intent on wielding ultimate power.

As part of Erdoğan's migrant-suppression programme,

agreed with the EU for €3 million euros, he also bargained for the Turkish people to get a free Schengen pass into Europe. Like a fastpass at Disneyland. This logic is effectively the same as importing chickens when you don't like eggs.

Erdoğan is precisely the sort of lunatic that stands up in public places and tells women to get shagging because the country needs more children and it is their job to push them out. Women are the incubators of a whole new generation of Muslims and they are expected to be the conduit to his grand plan: a world ruled by Muslim men.

Git.

But at least he looks dodgy. No part of me looks at him and thinks: 'Wouldn't say no.' He looks like an oily man whose sweat would taste slightly of olives and garlic and it's very likely he has sticky bollocks to boot. (Ladies will understand what I mean here. Men, if you don't, your partner is way too polite.)

However, there are other leaders who are far scarier. I present to you:

JUSTIN TRUDEAU

Justin Trudeau is the not-so-secret crush of all of Canada and most men in Alaska too. And Justin's number one fan is quite possibly Justin himself.

When I think of Justin, I see that he is the most highly evolved of all cunning politicians: ruthless, but covered with a human skin that is pleasing to the eye. If Sadiq Khan had sex with Emmanuel Macron and gave birth to a liberal-leftie baby, Trudeau would be the result.

This year he turned up at a Gay Pride event wearing special Ramadan socks to celebrate the fact it was also Eid (the end of Ramadan). For Christ's sake. The only way he could be more right-on is if he wore a pussy hat and an environmental banner at the same time – which I wouldn't put past him.

Trudeau is a big fan of migrants and open borders and outspoken in his disgust for Trump. So much so that the old Olympic stadium in Canada has been used as a temporary overflow centre for all the migrants hotfooting it from the US in pursuit of the American dream – or Canadian disaster.

The Canadians are a curious breed. Though not quite as artistically dysfunctional as the Germans, they do singularly lack any kind of personality or naughty streak. I imagine sex with a Canadian would be a dull and unadventurous affair, punctuated by apologies and courtesies at every turn.

Would you mind awfully if I poked this in there?

Which means that Trudeau the pin-up does absolutely nothing for me, even though power can generally make even the most unfortunate-looking of men unimaginably attractive, and cause beautiful women to ignore the fact they should never be seen first thing, last thing or without clothes.

At which point I give you:

FAT BOY KIM

While power works for some, it makes others – notably those who were undoubtedly megalomaniacs in the first place – truly repellent. Fat Boy Kim, better known as Kim Jong-un, is a good example. Clearly no woman is ever going to go near that thing voluntarily, so he has consigned himself to a life of killing his closest family members using anti-aircraft missiles, and eating cheese. Hard cheese at that.

In much the same way as in Margaret Atwood's *The Handmaid's Tale*, I imagine North Korean handmaids are dispatched to Fat Boy Kim's apartment from time to time so that he can stick in his chipolata and try to procreate.

By the time you're reading this jolly missive to your good self – by which I mean this book – on the bus or crowded train, with your face stuffed in someone's armpit, cursing the day Southern Rail was ever given a contract, Kim Jong-un may have been obliterated from existence after waving one too many nuclear warheads in the direction of Guam.

Or he'll still be waving nuclear warheads and Trump will have manifested some even bigger ones. In either case, the situation is not exactly stable.

SAUDI ARABIA

The Arab lands are not precisely the stuff of milk and honey, either. These are the lands that political correctness has passed by.

And it is here that the mystery of our Western feminists' blindness towards the mistreatment of women is most keenly felt; perhaps the shifting Arab sands get in their eyes.

In Saudi Arabia, women can only travel with a male relative; they cannot leave the country without permission from a senior male family member; have to keep themselves covered in public; and can be divorced if their husband simply mumbles 'I divorce you' three times over his cornflakes (or Arab equivalent). Women have very little or no representation and are forbidden from doing the most basic things that we enjoy. They can't drink, dance to music or have a right laugh with their mates while gadding about in a park with two bottles of prosecco. They are essentially baby-making machines and accessories under curtains.

Rich women are treated royally and permitted to smack their servants about. The less rich recognise sexual and domestic violence more than they recognise their own face in the mirror. Either way, daughters are the property of the family – their own or the family of the man they are going to marry, sometimes chosen for them before they are six years old.

And yet, despite the fact that Saudi women are told how to think, dress, walk and talk, and that their role in life is to be their husband's possession, our liberal feminists have nothing to say about it.

Nothing. Silence. Nada. Het.

Nothing to say about the burka. Nothing much to say about FGM. Nothing to say about a lack of representation in any body of power.

It is the cruellest of paradoxes.

Sweden's feminist mafia decided to visit Saudi and the picture of them smothered in fabric and material to hide their seemingly emancipated selves from the Saudi men was vomit-inducing. Where did all their aggressive female empowerment go?

If the participants in the women's marches really want to achieve something, they should leave the streets of nice metropolitan places with good transport links and instead get their naked arses to Saudi and parade about with their breast-icles on display. Or lie topless across the Saudi embassy lawn.

If it is equality women are after, why do they only shout about equality for Western women? And even then, when they do shout, their righteousness only applies within narrow parameters, to Christian women, and remains subservient to the hierarchy of group-thought, wherein welcoming migrants and multiculturalism matters more than the rights of women not to be raped on New Year's Eve in a public square.

BRITAIN'S BURKAS

I am not a huge fan of the special emissaries sent from Saudi to shop exclusively at Selfridges or on Bond Street, New Bond Street or Park Lane. I still baulk at the sight of women in full burkas and face veils in London, no matter how often I see them. And when they are carrying bags filled with Western paraphernalia – shoes and handbags and nonsense – I clench my teeth and shake my Western head.

What is it with these women who come here and blatant-ly refuse to integrate with our culture and our dress but are willing to sharp-elbow their way to the front of the Selfridges queue to ensure they get their scoop of Western goods to take home? What do they do with these items – wear them at home? Parade them about in front of their mates in private?

What's the point of Manolo Blahniks in private if outside your house you dress like a molehill on the move? Frankly it gets my goat. Not because of religion. Not because of Islam. And not because of men.

But because this is not the way of women. Women are better than this. We are too cool to be hidden under a curtain. And if blokes can't help but look at you, then you go, girlfriend. Give him something to be jealous of. Don't hide it all away so the fat, rich git your father made you marry (along with four other women) can line you up like one of his idiot supercars and feel better about his flaccid penis.

Nothing about the behaviour of Arab men does it for me. I simply could never connect. Their culture runs deep in their bones. And their culture is as antiquated as the square wheel.

THE SINAI PENINSULA

About as unstable as my mother-in-law, the Sinai Peninsula is a positive oasis for jihadists only waiting for an afternoon off to come thundering up the beach you are tanning yourself on, with an automatic weapon and the need to kill as many infidels as possible.

Any holidaymaker who books a cheap holiday in Sharm El Sheikh is utterly mad. Clearly nothing the Foreign Office nor I can say will convince them that a safe holiday somewhere more expensive, which they will actually survive, is better than a cheap holiday from which they might never return.

It is a curious thing. After skin cancer came along, we used to say people were dying for a tan. Now they literally are. At the hands of jihadists. And yet they still book.

THE FALKLANDS

British territory.

If you are young and about to argue that we have no business owning land that is nowhere near our country – that's called geography. Not politics. You are in the wrong class. Go out, shut the door behind you and never come back.

Admiral Sir John Forster Woodward, Task Force commander for the Falklands War, delivered the manliest lines ever uttered on the face of the planet: 'People will die, ships will be lost, that's the deal. Go to it.' How great would he have been working in HR?

If you don't understand why the Falklands belongs to the British, you were quite clearly never a fan of Thatcher or the Marines. And if you don't want to take the word of a horse-faced twat-bag, then how about you go and ask the Falkland islanders who they want to be governed by? Ninety-eight per cent say the UK. And that should be good enough for both of us.

GERMANY

Definitely on the spectrum and devoid of any emotional intelligence, Germans are the opposite of everything I am. And Angela Merkel is the perfect example.

That woman could murder both her parents with an ice pick in the middle of the night and still be in Brussels in a pant suit by 7 a.m., ready to talk about disputed fishing territories off the Cornish coast.

Germany scares me. Germans scare me. I didn't even like my German teacher back in school.

And I know we aren't supposed to mention the war, but I mention it in my head all the time and it makes me smile.

Did you know, Angela Merkel travels with a wardrobe

assistant specifically tasked to make her look boring so people focus on her politics and not what she is wearing?

God only knows how she ever got married.

SOCIALISM

I am sure socialism sounds great when you can afford it. If you are a red-hot liberal living inside zones 1 to 4 in London, have a cushy public-sector job, are linked to power, and are generally only two or three doors removed from the centre of things, socialism probably sounds great.

Of course everyone else in the world should have equal access to stuff, all schooling should be available to everyone, and at no point should Daddy ever hold open a door to help you get your foot in and give you a shunt up the greasy pole.

I wouldn't mind that as a position except for the fact that every single one of the blighters lecturing to this point has themselves benefited from one of the things they want to take away from the rest of us.

Take James O'Brien as a case study. He is a left-wing presenter at the radio station where I used to work, LBC. He is also a presenter for BBC's *Newsnight*. And has his fingers in multiple other establishment pies.

He is the ultimate socialist, bewailing private schooling, the inequalities of life and the hardships suffered by those on low incomes. He is a terrific supporter of open borders and the free movement of people, a vehement Remainer, and a big believer in equal access for all.

What he doesn't add to his endless lectures across the airways are the details of his own set-up. I know the figure on his paycheck, and it would make you fall off your perch in disgust.

He is a privately educated boarding-school boy who was given his first opportunities in media by his own father, a respected columnist for the *Telegraph*. And he lives among the inescapable privilege of central London.

Which is all fine and good with me. I do not begrudge him these things. In fact, accumulation of wealth according to the free market is precisely the creed I follow. But I do not understand how you can blatantly enjoy all the privileges of a certain type of life, and yet seek to deny others access to them.

If you live a life of isolated privilege, with access to doctors, private health, private schooling and excellent transport and employment opportunities, don't pretend you are a man of the people or that you are in any position to lecture the 'rest of the UK, who actually have to compete with all-comers for anything', about how to think.

Why do Labour MPs speak out against private education, then choose it for their own children? (Diane Abbott.)

How can someone mock the Tory Party for nepotism but then install his own son in an agency? (Jeremy Corbyn.)

The hypocrisy is rife.

ISLAM

Islamophobia – the meaning of, not the practice of – must be on the curriculum in primary schools these days, along with the jolly phonics books that help you distinguish between curly C and kicking K, because it is one of the words most overused by the young people of today.

It works on the basis that labelling you a hater enables people to shut you down, and it's something I hear often.

A phobia is an irrational fear: spiders, heights, rubber gloves (I kid you not), small spaces.

My fear of Islam is rational, based on the simple fact that most men who want to blow up my children, run down my children, or stab my children with a twelve-inch hunting knife on one of London's bridges are, in fact, Muslims – no matter how skewed their interpretation of the religion is.

Like all sensible mothers, rather than risk finding out whether or not this spider is deadly by petting it to see if it bites, I prefer to avoid the spider all together.

I would, similarly, rather avoid Islam and everything about it. I don't want to live near it, grow up around it, or have it pervading my working or private life. I don't really mind what you call me because of this. You can call me horse-face, ugly, old, a bigot – go for it. Because any amount of labelling by you does not change me. And it certainly does not change the way I feel.

For a woman, Islam appears to have much in common with an abusive marriage. It does not let you out alone. It does not let you meet new people or go out wearing what you feel good in. It places restrictive rules around your life and how you live it. And if you try to leave it, it comes after you and attempts to kill you.

Anything that comes in the guise of an abusive marriage is not a religion to me. It is just another abusive relationship. Which is precisely how I see Islam.

The difference between dedicated Muslims and myself is

that I can absolutely respect they will feel differently to me. I don't need to kill them for loving their religion. I have no wish to silence their views if they speak out in favour of it.

And yet my views in my country see me placed under threat.

CATHOLICS

My dislike for Islam is not discriminatory, because I happen to think religion is the cause of most of the conflict and ill will in the world, so in some ways at least my views are more balanced than the BBC. Catholics are no better than Muslims.

My husband is a Catholic and his family is quite fiercely Catholic. And while they are all jolly nice, Catholics can be as evil and set on vengeance as the average drunk in the street.

When Mark and I first got together he was already married. One of his more hardcore Catholic relations in Australia was not overwhelmed with God's love and forgiveness. No, she was not. Instead she wrote a two-page missive (on tragic airmail paper) about how we would both burn in hellfire and had Satan in our souls.

My fiercely Catholic mate has a lesbian daughter and to this day cannot acknowledge her own daughter's sexuality.

This bothers me. It bothers me that a religion should dictate right or wrong, good or bad, who you do and don't sleep with. There are seemingly virtuous Catholics who are bitter and filled with malice and evil, and who use their religion as a weapon to beat up those they disagree with.

And how on earth can it be possible for a religion to demand celibacy? Why are sex and the Church always intertwined? No wonder there is such a problem with sex inside the Catholic Church, and all the sickening, covered-up incidents of paedo priests boffing legions of young choir boys.

Two places I don't want my kids to end up: Disneyland and church. I suspect there is an equally high concentration of paedos in both.

A wise man once alleged that all Abrahamic faiths are obsessed with sex as a way to control the most vulnerable in our society, a means by which to cast them all into hell.

I tend to agree.

SIKHS

For BBC staff, or the slightly simple folk who get confused when attaching images to articles or on social media, let me explain: Sikhs are the exceptionally cool-looking men and women who wear bright clothes and turbans. They are not Muslims. In fact, if there is an opposite of the Muslims, the Sikhs are probably it.

Essentially I am a one-woman Sikh fan club. It may be politically incorrect to say so, but I love all Sikhs, hug them unapologetically on sight and hope that if reincarnation turns out to be a thing, I come back as one.

It has to be said that a turban would cut down the cost and time associated with trying to actually have hair.

I encourage you to befriend a noble Sikh and champion any cause they support with every sinew of your being. And if there is ever anything useful I can do for my Sikh brothers or sisters, you know where I am.

JEWS

It should be pretty clear by now that I am an aspiring Jew. It is the cause of much consternation to me that I was born with this nose in the middle of my face but didn't get to be an actual, real-life Jew and join the party. It's like really loving tennis but being born with no arms. A royal pain in the arse.

Jews have the best time and run an enviable circuit of dinners, parties and festivities centred mainly around lights. And food. Which are two of my favourite things.

And they also love to make a big deal about Friday nights, which are the equivalent of a page break in your week, and vital for mental health.

They also have cool words for things that we don't have words for. The Jews have an entire lexicon to make them feel more special.

Yishar koach is you should have strength. *Bubbeleh* is sweetie pie or doll. And *farshtinkerneh* is stinky. I mean … what's not to love? It drives me *meshuganeh* (crazy/bonkers)!

Best of all, my Jewish mates have a cool disregard for the bits of Jewish life that their mothers-in-law think matter and they definitely don't; they just pretend to be fully hardcore Jewish when the in-laws are around. Out at the pub with me, they eat prawns and don't give a monkeys. But if their mother-in-law phones asking which is the milk pan, they know the right answer and can tell her. It strikes me that Jewish people pretend to be hardcore by owning a milk pan. Or not eating prawns.

Whereas Muslim people think being hardcore means

blowing up children at a concert or setting fire to commuters on the subway.

Many Jewish ladies wear a wig, to cover their own hair out of respect for their husbands, which is a right laugh and hugely time-efficient in the mornings. Bad hair day? No drama. Whack on a wig and off you go.

My lovely Jewish friend puts her Jewish wig on the small family dog so it can run about looking gorgeous.

I have ultimate respect for this kind of approach to religion. Less a bad marriage or abusive relationship than an exciting affair, full of code words, twinkling lights, glorious food and fabulous hair.

CHAPTER 6

WHAT DO YOU ACTUALLY DO?

To be fair, my mother asks this question on a fairly regular basis, given my job doesn't really have a title and I don't go to an office or wear a uniform.

I don't have a one-word title like 'doctor' to tell her she's been a parenting success. And I refuse to make something up like 'social activist' or 'full-time mummy' – both meaning unemployed.

One of my mates just celebrated her 23-year anniversary in her job, the same place she has worked since leaving university. My own father worked the same job his whole life, for the same firm, the South West Electricity Board – or SWEB to the locals. His brother worked for the same firm too, and they are the spitting image of each other. Where I come from, people get in and stay put. And risk-takers need not apply.

I have gone off grid. Way off grid.

I think I was born with itchy bones – like fat people say they are born with big ones. Clearly we're both talking absolute bollocks but like so many siblings of settled ones, I have never been able to sit still. And my little ramble through what made me and the lessons I learned while gallivanting about the planet schooling or working seem to be the exact thing I do now.

My official title on screens and TV is 'broadcaster and columnist'. I can't bring myself to say journalist, because it sounds too sensible and formal. I think I am a new breed of columnist, one that doesn't write her columns sat on her fat arse in her pyjamas in her kitchen (Sarah Vine, I'm looking at you) but actually bothers to go and have a look at the stuff she is talking about.

There are two types of columnist: great ones and crap ones. And I aspire to be the former. Rod Liddle is my hero. He is a quite brilliant man, makes me laugh out loud when I read him, is still teaching me words I didn't know existed, and can file vast swathes of copy on a weekly basis without once giving the game away that he was all the while running late for school pick-up and in a bit of a rush.

He also says the stuff I think and calls out the state and the system for the nonsense that it is. As such, of course, he takes his fair share of flak. He was the subject of some rancid investigation for something he inferred in a column, which later turned out to be true, about crime rates among non-UK citizens.

He has had his fair share of bruises. But he remains a champion. I worry for his future now that sponsors and advertisers are trying to signal their virtue via the content they sponsor.

India Knight is another. She is now removed from the merry hell that is London; I like to imagine her ankle-deep in farmyard muck caring only about whether her broccoli is sprouting as it should.

I love her column in the *Sunday Times Magazine*. And I love that each week she has something completely left-field to say, because she has committed the space and time in her head to think differently. If you ever feel you are going mad or your head is full, breathe deeply and read India Knight. Great name that, by the way.

Others are not so clever. Take Sarah Vine, the hideous wife of Michael Gove and flump-master general at the *Daily Mail*. When I picture her, it is with Mr Dacre's hand up her back, working her mouth, spitting out whatever editorial he wants.

If Paul Dacre (the *Daily Mail*'s editor) makes the paper about the legs of the Scottish First Minister and British Prime Minister, you can bet your last pound that within twelve hours Vine will be trotting out some cheap column about how women couldn't really give a stuff about their legs but if others want to compliment them, then fantastic. And it will get her a header on the front page.

She is essentially the figurative Monica Lewinsky of the *Daily Mail* office, having learned her art while fellating her husband's reportedly massive organ – which is apparently even bigger than his ego. Although I should point out that Monica Lewinsky is considerably better looking and has hair to die for. Unlike Vine, whose hair looks like it died a long time ago.

Vine is one of those 'I was born fat and have fat bones' idiots who cannot accept responsibility for their own size, preferring instead to blame my good self even as she stands in front of her own fridge (on a chair) shovelling food down her face.

I know she used to complain to my former editor that my columns did better than hers because he wrote better headlines for me. I mean, how childish can you get? Without her husband, I'd assert her relationship with the newspaper would be far more arms-length than at present.

There are other idle columnists too. They typically have one thing they fixate on in their own life and use this as material in every single column they write. So that week by week you are getting more and more minutiae about their small world. These are the true introspectives. They look inwards and see only themselves. Not outwards, considering their place in the bigger scheme of things.

Bryony Gordon is a perfect example. She has a mental illness and suffers from depression. And good on her for talking about it, writing about it, and making a living out of it. Kudos for that.

But, conversely, is there nothing else in your bloody life, love? Can you not park it and give it a rest for a bit? Yes, Prince Harry is brave and has struggled. Yes, young girls are under pressure and have eating disorders as a result; yes, all those pictures of skinny models are annoying for chubsters, and, absolutely, men need to be able to speak out if they are so pissed off with life that they are inclined to chuck themselves under a train.

(Particularly if it is my train and I am keen to get home. I don't mind people killing themselves, but for Christ's sake, can you do it somewhere else? Specifically not the 19.03 to the West Country. I have things to do and people to see. I am sad that your life is a bit shit. But mine is still quite busy.)

I look at her column but I can't bring myself to read it because it's always going to be about the same thing. Even if she was writing about *The Great British Bake Off* she'd still somehow make it about herself and her brave but chronic struggle with... everything. I am amazed her contract gets renewed. Then again, when I see the number of people who identify as mentally ill, I understand that hers is a lucrative business to be in.

There is no faster way to get booked to speak on a panel than to fess up to some kind of struggle.

Feminists are another columnist lens I find peculiar. It must be exhausting to view all of life through the goggles of an angry woman, cross at not being a man and determined that all men are arseholes.

Conducting a permanent whingeathon against all that is good about boys requires an acute lack of humour and, indeed, feminists never seem to laugh. They fail to make me laugh, too. Most are utterly disappointing.

The biggest single failure of female and feminist columnists is their disinclination to stand up and shout on behalf of women who need their voices to be heard. Feminists have a strict hierarchy of things that matter, and it cannot be inverted or overturned: girl power, multiculturalism, tolerance for minority groups, Jeremy Corbyn, anyone with an issue, environmentalism, all things LGBT, environmentalism and pork products in the new five pound note.

When there is mass child sexual exploitation across the UK (as there is) and children abused in every major city in the country (as there are) at the hands of a sophisticated, organised and relentless network of groomers (as there is), you won't hear so much as a squeak from the feminists.

White girls are not on their list. They are not a minority group (although I would argue that they are in Birmingham, Luton and Leicester) and they don't rank on the hierarchy. Multiculturalism and tolerance of Islam take precedence.

The same rule applies to LGBT rights. Normally, feminists will applaud and support the LGBT cause and are keen to be allied with PRIDE and other events that put them on the correct side of 'right-think'.

But in their weird game of Opinion Top Trumps, Islam is higher up the hierarchy than LGBT rights. So Islamic homophobia and Islam's outright rejection of gays, to the extent that they are thrown off tall buildings, are not discussed, even though, arguably, you are born gay but have to adopt a religion. They adhere to their right-think.

This hierarchy of views is madness and at times hugely frustrating. It's not that they are inconsistent; it's that they are hugely consistent in their inconsistencies. And happy with them, too.

I used to write my column two or three times a week for my boss. Unlike weekly columnists, who have to wait to see what lands near their day, I could pick up on the things that really got me thinking or made me cross or sad.

As a Friday columnist at *The Sun*, waiting to see what was around, then filing on Thursday for Friday, was a pain in the arse. You wait, wait, wait, miss the things you want to shout about, and then have one day to create your worldview on whatever's left, trying to avoid repetition or boring the reader senseless.

On occasion, in the early days, I failed spectacularly. I remember taking one particular call from the lovely lady who hired me and was the conduit of truth between the big boss and me. She told me he didn't like it.

I asked, which bit?

All bits. He had redlined the whole thing.

One of the key tips for column writing is to write it as you think it, and to write like you speak. The moment you try to make things beautiful or try to be clever or construct the thing like a collage, you are stuffed.

I remember calling Lovely Mark to have a weep about how my boss had hated it, how mortified I was that I hadn't done well, and then sitting in some godforsaken café trying to rewrite a whole new column in two hours.

I can still remember the piece; it was about Tom Daley, the diver. He had just made the big announcement that he was gay and had officially come out in a video, which I think he posted to YouTube. Right-think was clearly that this was a very brave thing to do and he should be applauded for leading the way so that another wave of gay sportsmen and women could be honest, too.

Which I get.

But I couldn't help thinking that Tom Daley coming out was a little less brave than, let's say, a 24-stone rugby player exiting the closet – probably through the side panel face first.

If your career essentially involves jumping about in a very small pair of pants in front of a legion of women who enjoy cross-stitch and the Women's Institute, your audience is a) not going to be surprised that you're gay, and b) likely to be understanding and kind about it.

I never completely understand why people have to come out about anything any more. Everyone is so busy coming out all over the place, with more issues than Vesuvius. Quite frankly, I'd be more surprised if someone decided to stay in and keep themselves to themselves.

Instead they tell me they have their period and isn't it outrageous there is a tampon tax. Or they have chronic depression and couldn't get out of bed. Or have HIV but are positive about their future.

I mean, Jesus Christ, people. You can have a private life, you know. I am a vaguely heterosexual woman who once got diagnosed with early-stage genital warts; I have never felt the need to come out about it on YouTube.

Aside from my column writing, I am a pretty decent radio talk-show host. At least, I was until one unfortunate tweet, using language I regret, gave my political and media adversaries the ammunition to get me booted off the air.

My contract says I agreed to leave, so I imagine that I'd better leave it at that. Except that I would much prefer to have agreed to stay, and in fact I just had, three months before, by signing a new twelve-month contract.

Mine was the fastest-growing Sunday radio show and it was ripping chunks out of BBC Radio 5 live in the ratings war, so I am sure that whichever dastardly network conspired to get me removed, the BBC and *The Guardian* were pleased with their efforts.

I had already received a warning that my removal was being planned at high levels; a journalist and free-speech fan inside *The Guardian*, an insider at the morning conference with Katharine Viner (the boss at *The Guardian*), had emailed me to let me know the plan was to take me down.

I was grateful for the support. And the support of so many people who wrote, emailed and tweeted to say they were sorry to see me go.

It was pretty emotional at times; I loved that show. And I think it might have been the first time we have seen someone relatively high-profile be silenced so swiftly by an aggressive campaign from the left.

I miss it. I will be back. And I hope to bring my lovely listeners with me.

Talk radio is a brilliant thing. Terrifying at first, but awesome once you've got it. I imagine it to be a bit like flying a helicopter, without the threat of actually being killed if you go wrong and crash, or the need to spend six years getting advanced training just to get the whirring thing airborne.

And, of course, the jumpsuit is optional.

But in terms of doing a thousand things at once while keeping cool, it's pretty much up there.

There is just you, the headphones and the mic. Anything that happens in those two hours is all on you. Two hours of empty air that you are required to fill, with callers chatting about subjects you hope they will want to talk about.

What if no one rings in? What if no one is listening? What if everyone thinks these topics are dull as hell and would rather go and do the gardening? What if you have a heart attack live on air?

These are the early nightmares you need to be able to put in a box. There are bigger nightmares, too. What if the Queen dies when I am live on air? What if there is a massive news story that is sad and serious? What if I have a funny turn and take all my clothes off? And there are the little nightmares. How will I get to the news on time if this guy doesn't shut up? Which button was I supposed to press again? How do I pronounce the name of the news presenter I am supposed to know and who will take it really bloody personally if I get it wrong *again*?

There are a multitude of things to be aware of. There is the producer talking in your ear, until you make a face that says shut up. There is a talk-back screen where your producer can write stuff for you to say, or help you cover your arse if you have stuffed up, or stick up the number for the Samaritans if listeners suddenly feel suicidal.

Then there is the text screen, where listeners' texts flood in and where you can select, click and drag individual messages into your folder to read out. Reading out texts is a great way of enabling shy people to be heard. In the case of dull presenters, it's also a way to fill time in the absence of any real people to talk to. Splendid.

And then there is the Twitter feed on a separate screen. If you understand Twitter, and particularly my Twitter, which can be pretty fierce, you will understand that the Twitter feed can be fairly rude. Well, OK: very rude.

'Hopkins, you big-nosed twat, get off the bloody air.'

'What is this rancid cow bleating on about?'

'Will someone assassinate this stupid white whore bag before I go in and kill her myself.'

This was the kind of running commentary I could expect while I was trying to hold an uplifting phone-in about

Theresa May's decision to call a snap election – as ill-fated as that turned out to be.

Two phone lines to play with, a call screen filled with waiting callers, a text screen, a Twitter screen, a talk-back screen and a producer in your ear. Then there was the social media team asking you to talk into camera – and all on top of having a radio show to run.

In an ideal world you would take your listeners on a journey through the hour, moving through the topic so you aren't just waffling on about the same old stuff, or getting repeat callers who ring in to agree with what the last caller just said.

Then there are the broader issues.

Ofcom is pressed up against the radio like a paedophile at a primary school when I am on air. They get hard just hoping for a glimpse of something they can complain about, or even thinking about all the liberal letters of complaint fluttering down on their heads like tenners on the poor.

There were also my bosses and their weird crushes. George Michael, for example. Now, I love George more than anyone. My first single was by Wham. And I am super sad that George died.

But his death was not worthy of two hours of radio on a Sunday, especially not after three hours gamely provided by the bloke who went before me, and non-stop bulletins every fifteen minutes from the poor sod of a reporter dispatched to stand outside George's cottage.

I told the bosses I was not doing two bloody hours of dead George Michael. They told me they were disappointed I had not been able to find a way to make it work.

In a more strategic sense, my purpose was to give the

listeners an opportunity to at least hear another side of any given argument – to give the rest of the country a voice.

After liberal bleeding hearts 24/6 I thought two hours on the seventh wasn't too much to ask.

During my time on radio we had Brexit and Trump; I couldn't have asked for a better time to be on air.

The real leftie liberals couldn't even bring themselves to speak to me. I believe one producer wrote a blog telling me to fuck off. James O'Brien refused to let me fill his shift when he was on holiday, despite my being booked to do so, and one of the most viewed clips from LBC, of me ranting about Brexit, was mysteriously deleted from Facebook by one of the social media team.

People speak about the shock of my sacking. The bigger shock was me managing to endure such a hostile culture for so long, and still manage to increase listener numbers.

After I left, my lovely social media manager left too, having been overlooked for a better role in favour of a less experienced bloke. Something tells me that place is allergic to women. And I am more manly than most and deeply trans-racial at the weekends.

But I am not too bitter about it. I learned a new skill and I loved it. Speaking to people as they pad about their kitchens in their pyjamas, cooking the Sunday roast, was a privilege. Hearing people share their most secret selves live on air, telling stories they would never normally repeat in public, was a complete honour.

I am just deeply sad to have left. I miss it – like a friend or a home you loved. Not the station, not the other presenters (Jesus) and not the publicity. I miss my listeners and our chats.

The programmes leading up to my dismissal, on grooming gangs and child sexual exploitation, were the best I have done. Not in any professional radio sense, I am sure, but those shows, the ladies who came on, the girls who shared their stories and were heard – I think that mattered. And I am proud of all that.

It is a curious thing that once more the liberals were able to close me down right after the weeks I spent on child-grooming gangs and the rape of white girls. It's a pattern repeated across the media over and over again. Even the Labour MP Sarah Champion was forced to resign after writing a balanced piece for *The Sun* on grooming gangs. There is something sinister at play here, involving the media, the establishment and the police. And I do not flinch from talking about it. And I will not flinch from finding out in the future. I am determined to get back on air. I look forward to chatting with my lovely listeners again.

There are three types of radio phone-in caller I love.

1. ANGRY MAN WITH STRONG REGIONAL ACCENT
Unbeatable. The angrier a person gets, the stronger their accent. So if they start raging at you in a strong, barely comprehensible Irish accent, you can guarantee when they have reached peak rage, only their closest family members will have a clue what they are blathering on about. Only key swear words can be understood.

This is no bad thing and it breaks the monotony of softly spoken ladies from Wimbledon.

2. STAUNCH MUSLIMS CONVINCED I AM ISLAMOPHOBIC

Angry Muslims make for classic calls. I had two or three pet angry Muslim callers who, when I was on air and in need of a diversion, a little break or some change in tempo, could be summoned up from their prayer mats to launch an industrial-scale assault on The Hopkins.

There is something curious about deeply religious people calling you a monster, an evil demon, a witch of a woman, and hoping only bad things happen to you. It has the slightly genius effect of engendering support for me and my right to speak in more moderate Muslims and women who do not enjoy hearing a woman being called names live on air by a man.

And I pay not the slightest bit of attention to the abuse. So, in a way, everyone was a winner. The caller felt better, I felt in control of my radio show, and the abuse garnered me support.

3. FIRST-TIME FEMALE CALLERS

When someone calls in for the first time, I think it is a big thing. A really big thing. They have taken the time to get the number, make space in their life to call, and, bigger still, buck up the courage to call in live on air and risk sounding silly.

These fears aren't unique to women, but they are hugely more common among women. Women's default position is that they are going to sound stupid, or be made to look stupid, and that that will be mortifying – and difficult to recover from.

It is never the case. First-time female callers, so determined to have their point heard that they will defy the huge risk of personal shame they believe they are exposing themselves to, are inevitably quite brilliant.

If it is you, I applaud you. You are queens. And every time you call, you are articulating the views of another thousand women who couldn't quite bring themselves to take the risk that day. Which is completely understandable too.

It's the reason the voices you hear on most shows are predominantly male. Or the same small set of female callers. Because unless you offer up an access point and the commitment to help people have their voice heard, you are immediately silencing half of your audience.

Women on the radio are always there banging on about idiotic female issues – like maternity or childcare. It is so patronising, I can hardly bear it. Hello, 1970s? This is modern women calling.

Women are brilliant at talking about politics and the intersection between it and their families. They are just not given the time and space to do so.

The liberals silence regular women spectacularly well. By acting like they know it all, being actively prepared to condemn callers as idiots, and failing to grant a point of entry for women whose default belief is that they will sound stupid, they miss so many listeners and callers.

I love these women – and men – who, despite their fears,

are determined to have their voices heard. I admire them and respect them.

The list of dreadful callers best avoided is far longer. You can usually tell within three words that a call is headed south. It was a cause of some tension between me as a presenter and the team behind the glass if they put through utter dullards who contributed less to the debate than a dumb mute with chronic ulceration of the mouth.

These are some of the people on my dreadful-caller list.

1. REPEAT CALLER/STALKER OBSESSIVE

Some callers believe they are actually having a relationship with you. They give themselves a nickname and refer to past calls, suggesting you will remember them. They are like a weird stalker boyfriend who you never actually dated but who has pictures of you in his wallet.

2. EXTREME RELIGIOUS TYPES WHO THINK THE ANSWER IS GOD, EVEN IF THE QUESTION IS WHY ALL FEMALE LEADERS ARE CHILDLESS

Usually they will tell you it is all in God's plan, whether you are discussing the ethnic cleansing of the Yazidi people or the rise of sexually transmitted disease in the over-forties.

I have no problem with people who think that everything can be explained by God. But if your faith is that entrenched and your belief that deep, I am unlikely to be able to challenge them during a two-minute conversation live on air. Or find a rational tenet of your belief to pick a hole in. So you win. God is Top Trumps. And I ain't playing.

3. ASTROLOGISTS

Ditto the above, except they believe the explanation for the inability of the British establishment to accept Brexit lies in the alignment of Saturn and Mars, and the fullness of the moon.

While it is fascinating that some individuals live their lives in happy acceptance that the stars are controlling everything – a position I rather admire – it doesn't lend itself to a healthy mid-morning debate.

I do respect these people, though. Imagine living life so utterly delegating responsibility for anything and everything to the solar system! If you wake up butt naked in a field with a kitchen implement up your arse and a vague recollection you were supposed to collect your kids at 4 p.m. yesterday, but you went to the bar instead – you can explain it all away because Jupiter was circling Uranus and you were helpless in its power. Sterling stuff.

4. GRUDGE CALLERS

Let's say you are a chubster whom I have offended in the past. It might be that today's topic is the geopolitical uncertainties facing west Africa. Regardless of that fact, you are going to ring me and start ranting that I am an idiot because I once said you were fat because you ate too many doughnuts. This is no problem and I am happy to let you vent, but it does rather throw us off topic and make the hour sound odd.

One moment we were talking about contraceptive clinics on the Ivory Coast; the next, fat Brenda from Brentford is calling me a cow for fat-shaming her and her fat friends. It's pretty hard to segue smoothly back from that.

But radio remains my big love. And I will be back. I am determined. I will update you via Twitter.

Which probably accounts for about 20 per cent of my time.

Many people, including former bosses, current bosses, legal teams, police, husbands and critics, have told me to STAY THE FUCK OFF TWITTER, usually in the shouty voices normally reserved for small children or dogs.

My own boss at Mail Online virtually destroyed my left ear drum shouting abuse at me for daring to wear a Trump 'Make America Great Again' hat after Charlottesville.

And, of course, they have a point. Twitter has been a source of much expense, tension, infighting and disruption in my working life.

I accept that Twitter is a failing platform, crassly censored in the worst possible way, and funded by Saudi influencers who silence dissenting voices. The speed and effectiveness of the Twitter machine and its ability to control the volume and flow of its content is kind of terrifying. Censorship is rife.

And it is true that I am not good at doing what I am told. And it is also true that Twitter has cost me dearly. When so many people are out to shut me down, it is not all that great when I give them a perfect excuse to do so.

But I will continue to acknowledge that the line I walk is very fine. It is a thin line, which I will invariably cross. And that will cost me. But the line is made fine by PC nonsense.

I will not make myself more polite just to please people or keep my job or keep advertisers happy.

I always knew I would be fired from my radio post one day; that's well documented. Any job is only ever a chapter in your life, and as long as you move purposefully to the next, you are stronger for the experience. But I would rather speak my mind than hold my tongue and keep my job, no matter how painful.

My followers are pushing close to a million, but my stalkers are probably double that or more, and they are the true powerhouses. The liberal media that stalk my Twitter feed but cannot shame themselves into following me are my keenest audience.

And as they sit in the shadows watching to protect their reputations, my feed and my content help shape what they write, for good or bad. And that is a powerful thing.

I love the immediacy of Twitter, the ability to build volume and apply pressure, and the platform it gives others who feed me information I can use to best advantage, whether it's about exposing police bias or student brainwashing on campus.

I am proud of my Twitter platform, and protective of it. I am not frightened by it, despite the obvious pain it has caused my career and my pocket.

In many ways, this is where I identify with those people willing to leave all responsibility to God or astrophysics; I do believe the Twitter world is slightly out of my control. Still, it's better to live big and talk loudly than be PR'd to death and become a fantasy of what an actual person thinks.

Being authentic means I will also be fired. And if I can't accept that, I do need to get the fuck off Twitter.

Happily for me and for my followers and legions of liberal stalkers, I do accept that. I am the Jesus of the outspoken. I will be martyred for my voice. But I will rise again. And if I don't, I will retire to Cornwall and nurse battery hens back to life.

I love my family, my children and living epilepsy free.

All these things are good.

Lesson 1: if you can be hired and fired with the same good grace, and move purposefully to your next endeavour, you will be strengthened by the experience. Doing one job for twenty years is admirable. Doing ten jobs for two is a whole lot more fun.

Lesson 2: life is not a straight-line graph. Mine has been more of a pinball experience, flicked and battered from pillar to post. But we're all spat out the same end.

Lesson 3: your life is made of many different bits. Work. Play. Sex. Rest. Exercise. Learning. Find which bits make you the happiest, and do them more often.

CHAPTER 7

THE THINGS THEY DO
TO SHUT YOU UP

Some people describe me as a controversialist, a shock jock, earning cash by saying offensive stuff that makes you want to lob a brick at your TV, things that will earn me attention. Like a small child.

I think that's just another way of trying to put me in a box and shut me up. Far easier to imagine this is all an act than to believe people actually hold the views I do, or to realise how many British people are sick of not being able to say how they feel. Far easier to imagine I am a monster and no 'normal' people think like I do – at least some of the time.

I have my own views on what a controversialist looks like – and I have met a few. They arrive on the scene from nowhere and disappear just as fast.

Do you remember Josie Cunningham? The woman got a pair of double Ds on the NHS and then became a glamour model and scored a place on the sofa at *This Morning* to talk about it.

She went on to do more shocking controversial stuff. She

sold tickets for the birth of her baby in her lounge, and invited the newspapers along for the ride.

And so it went on. Each act more desperate than the last to garner attention and cash.

One thing you can guarantee about these types, who I feel a bit sorry for, is there is always a weaselly 'agent' not far behind them, willing to sacrifice them on the altar of cash-for-clicks.

Weaselly agents are always unfeasibly small, wear cheap leather jackets, and can be found during normal hours working as part of the clean-up team in the aisles of ASDA.

I went to interview Josie for *The Sun* and was bored in an instant.

This is not true of all tabloid fodder. Many of these broken souls – known for their dramatic private lives, multiple marriages, divorces, breakdowns or a collapsed nose from snorting too much of the white stuff – are deeply fabulous and by far the most interesting people to sit and gossip with.

I genuinely believe it is the layers of life that give the depth of character that make us fascinating. And those who have been battered along the way are the best people to sit next to at weddings, because they have plenty to say and aren't afraid of saying it.

Nothing is more boring than Miss Perfect Pants who has been married to the same guy all her life, has paid off her mortgage by forty-five and has a perfect child (or two) busy being perfect and winning all the medals in school.

You know very well that out of perfect parents only mischief and Machiavellian mayhem can come. Their perfect Flora-May will probably end up drug-addled and legs akimbo as a bride of ISIS before she is fifteen. It's the natural order of life, which stops the perfect from being too terrific and gives us plebs something to gossip about. Given our own battered state, it enables us to embrace their fallen daughter as one of our own.

Since I still have a voice twelve years after *The Apprentice*, I'd argue there must be something more going on with me than being controversial. Or making a name for myself by selling my tits after wasting taxpayers' cash.

(My husband reminds me I would only get about £2.50 for my boobs on a good day. Although, since I stopped taking my epilepsy meds, they have put on quite a growth spurt and I have ambitions of being at least a B cup before I am fifty. I digress.)

If I am asked what I do, I say I am a columnist, regardless of which newspaper owner is enduring my presence – be it Murdoch or Lord Rothermere, I have my opinions and I share them. And I think I am still in work because I connect with ordinary people who have probably thought similar stuff to me at some point, but have not had the pleasure of saying it in public.

They probably say it to their mates, or in private to their spouses, but nowhere else.

'My dad loves you,' is pretty common. Or 'My mum thinks you are great.'

We get along because we are all living the same kinds of lives – normal lives. We're just people trying to bump along happily with our families. People who get together at Christmas and usually want to kill our sister-in-law. Whose mum is doing our head in at the moment because she is so dammed stubborn. Whose husband cannot seem to empty the washing machine, just opens the door to stop the beeping, as if that sorted anything. Whose kids think they are entitled to everything because maybe we have made it all too easy for them, and the worst thing we can do is disconnect the WiFi.

I am just one of these regular people. I am the person next to you on the bus or the train.

Although, it has to be said, I am finding buses harder these days. I have a bit of a thing about windows being open for fresh air and ventilation, and when you get that misty cloying air bogging up the windows I get a bit of a gag on and start retching.

If the person next to me has greasy hair or is sporting yesterday's tracksuit with that fusty smell of old bums, I am all but done.

Bus mums always have the crappiest kids. There are loads of them, inevitably ugly and a bit thick, who spend their ride squabbling, shouting or screaming. And you look at the mother and know that the kids don't stand a chance in hell of getting a single GCSE.

I was on a bus taking my daughter and her mates to a trampoline park the other day, and the adults of the family behind us appeared to be speaking in growling vowel sounds only, while their mutant offspring spoke in sniff and spits. I fear for the children of the bus people.

I am perhaps disappointingly normal and average. I just say out loud the stuff some of us think some of the time.

The weird thing is, the space to say these things out loud

is getting smaller and smaller. The list of things you aren't allowed to say is absolutely longer than the list of things you can.

Many of my listeners and readers prefer not to say what they think in public or on Twitter because they simply can't be doing with the hassle of the reaction from do-gooders. There is an obvious tick-list of the thoughts considered right and wrong, a checklist for life; some opinions are permitted, and some are not.

If you want an easy life, or to signal to others you are one of the 'acceptable voices', all you need do is trot out the list of correct opinions and you are in.

Which is strange when you think about it. Because surely everyone has a right to their opinion and a space in which to defend it?

It seems to me that we should not all share the same view otherwise we start to operate a bit like North Korea, and that is patently mad.

The BBC is the chief perpetuator of this group-think. At least North Korea gets its propaganda for free; we're obliged to pay for ours for the next ten years.

If we cannot hear the opinions of others who think differently, how can we understand the choices and decisions they make?

It is utter madness to me, for example, that any half-normal person would choose not to eat meat, to live dairy-free, or to declare they are gluten-free at a restaurant.

Coming from a dairy-farming background and having grown up knee-high in shit and afterbirth, I think living as a vegan, vegetarian or gluten-free pescatarian is a perversion and a direct result of having so few real problems in your life that you have to make some up.

When you run out of first-world problems and need to make some up, you probably need a new job. Or a better hobby. Or better sex. Or sex with someone other than yourself.

I have never known a homeless ex-serviceman tell me he is gluten-free when I offer to buy him a sarnie. Or ask for a soy milk chai latte when I offer him a coffee.

I've been forced to live with gluten-free individuals at times and have watched them revel in the extra attention it brings from staff and waiters. If you are gluten-free, why not sod off to a restaurant specially designed for your issues? Don't come out to normal restaurants and persecute the rest of us with your need to feel special.

Try living in Yemen. See how long you remain pescatarian.

I wonder how we reached a point where there are only right answers to the questions of life, as if life were an exam and someone made liberals the invigilators.

I struggle with the word liberal. It really slid on to the scene during the battle for Brexit, in the run-up to the referendum.

We were the Brexiteers. And the Remain team were the liberals, the liberal elite, the intelligent ones. Brendan Cox and his cronies at Hope Not Hate jumped on board like ticks on a dog and tried to own hope as well. So that everything perpetuated by liberals or Remainers was hope, and everything else was hate.

If you are ever bored on a Sunday afternoon, take a look into the power players, media connections, political and religious organisations and funding at Hope Not Hate and astonish yourself.

I wrote column after column setting out the stand of us against them. The rest of the UK against London. Normal folk against the rich of zone 1 and 2. The hardworking versus the liberal elite. And so it went on and the word liberal stuck.

Until we all worked out liberal was the wrong word for a bunch of people – typically wealthy people living in splendid isolation, or students sufficiently insulated from the realities of life and the rough of the road – who have a prescriptive way of thinking. A dictatorship of thought.

At which point, of course, the idea of liberal thinking, of being open to anything and accepting of most things, becomes the opposite of what you're saying.

The term liberal fascism has evolved out of Sean Hannity and the Fox News teams in America in response to the backlash against the Trump presidency and the silencing of conservatives.

And I think it is the best term we have to describe these people: liberal fascists, who would rather suppress free speech than face an alternative view. Who would rather insult than listen and refute. And who will fight rather than discuss calmly.

Antifa is the pinnacle of this hypocrisy: protesters calling themselves anti-fascists, who gather to protest against Conservative governments, policies and perceived injustices. These antifa protestors are funded, organised and uniformed in black with gas masks and face masks.

Having watched riots in a number of cities across the

world, I now see how these things start. And it is always with disgruntled kids who have never had to fight anything real in their lives, who want their chance at having a platform and attention for their thoughts – so they set fire to cars. I have worked with individuals able to get me tip-offs of where and when cars would be torched to guarantee press attendance at the 'mayhem' and coverage of their acts.

These liberal fascists have grown in strength and sophistication.

They want to close down debate, to control thinking. They stand for a return to the kind of socialism where everyone is equally poor.

Brexiteers, Conservatives, commentators like me are the opposite of these liberal fascists. We are tolerant Conservatives, strong on law and order, against intolerant Democrats who are united by a curiosity of causes from global warming to trans bathrooms.

As I write I am watching a Twitter storm appearing on my horizon. A Labour union leader has reported me to the Met Police for a tweet I wrote in the aftermath of another terror attack in London near Whitehall.

I tweeted that on that one day alone, there had been a bomb in France, a shooting in Germany and a knife attack in London, and added, for good measure, that Ramadan had not even started yet, and these sods get angry when they're hungry.

He reported this to the Met Police and within seconds they asked him to direct message them with details.

This Twitter conversation went global. And it is shocking on so many levels.

Shocking that *at the same moment* as a man is arrested for carrying knives outside our Parliament, a group of police are responding to lame-arsed tweets from someone with a clear political agenda.

Shocking that our response to actual terror on the streets is to investigate a tweet. Shocking that we actually have police dedicated to this nonsense. And shocking that in a country rapidly descending into chaos, the establishment puts finance behind an extremely limited set of variables within its control – social media being one of them.

It horrifies me. And sickens me.

I am very happy to be policed by Twitter itself. If Twitter wants me to take stuff down, or objects to how I use its platform, I can listen or be booted off. But the notion that this is actual police work is bonkers.

And if you argue that ISIS should not be on Twitter, you are absolutely right. And Twitter itself has a responsibility to get a grip on that, too.

But, of course, this is not the first attempt to silence me. It will not be the last. I have quite the history of being silenced by various means.

In her book *The Silencing*, Kirsten Powers writes about how, in the US, the left have worked their way across education, the political system, law and the judiciary to silence dissenting views and stifle debate.

We should be under no illusion: it is happening here, too.

Let's leaf through just a few of my experiences to help show what life is like when I do what I do.

SILENCING ON UNIVERSITY CAMPUSES

I used to be inundated with requests to talk at universities as part of their debating society programmes. Usually solo, sometimes as part of a panel discussion. With some vague notion of civic duty, I would try to do one talk per quarter as part of my commitment to encourage young people to have the balls to stand up and say what they think.

Or at least to show them other views than the ones they are prescribed by their liberal fascist lecturers on campus.

I want them to have the strength to stand up for their beliefs, whatever they are. Frankly I am not that bothered if someone is an anti-Israeli Marxist who wants Islamic Studies to be the only subject taught. I don't even mind if someone thinks Theresa May is the devil incarnate and I am the biggest threat to the security of the UK today.

I am content to listen to your argument, whoever you are, as long as you can imagine the possibility of listening to mine.

I was invited to talk at University College London in April 2016. I had dislocated an arm the night before with an epileptic fit, but managed to get it put back in at A&E during the night and then travel four hours to the university. If there is one thing I hate, it is being beaten by my weakness.

I was invited to the campus by the vice-chancellor. The student union had already tried to prevent me from coming to the campus and had organised a protest to have me disinvited or no-platformed in order to prevent me speaking.

What they didn't know was that I was working behind the scenes with the PR team to figure out how we could let the students have their little protest and carry on with the engagement anyway. And eventually we made it.

The students decided the way to no-platform me was to censor. And saw fit to allow me to make the four-hour trip, unpaid, to try to talk to them.

I was warned when I arrived that the students were still planning a protest, a walk-out five minutes into my talk. I was glad of the warning. Glad to be prepared. Forewarned is forearmed and all that.

I was offered the opportunity not to talk but decided that would be cowardice. After all, why let the actions of the few dictate how I approach life? If I allowed them to silence me or allowed my pride to dictate my actions, then whatever happened to my whole purpose on university campuses as I see it – which is to encourage students to stand strong?

As anticipated, the students stood up as soon as I started talking and left, en masse. They filmed themselves leaving (true to form for generation snowflake, who can't just do something, but must always be seen to be doing something). And then they all gave each other a cheeky blowie and a snog for being so clever. (They didn't. I made that bit up.)

The Muslim students on campus, who appeared to act much the same way as the Mafia, co-ordinated the whole stunt, and loved it. They controlled who came on campus and ensured Israeli produce did not. For them, Israeli mangoes were symbols of an oppressive regime. I was equally welcome. Me and Israeli mangoes. Equally terrifying for Muslim kids on campus.

The liberal fascists thought it was genius.

The students celebrated their utter brilliance as they stood around outside, comparing the bits they'd filmed on their phones wondering what to do next. And the rest of the panel carried on talking.

I was struck that I wasn't too bothered about it myself. Whether anyone stays to listen to me or not, I keep talking. They exercised their right to leave, even if they had only turned up to leave. I actually felt sorry for the rest of the panel who had inadvertently lost their audience.

However, I found out later via Twitter and emails from students with an ounce of decency that one of the panellists, a lecturer at that very university, had encouraged the students in their walk-out and congratulated them on 'making a stand'.

And this is what we are up against. I believe most university campuses are the prime instigators of liberal fascist thinking in our young people.

It is no coincidence that Corbyn and the left want to change things so that every vaguely literate person can go to university without fees and come out with a dodgy 2:1 in psychology before they hit the ranks of the unemployed.

Brainwashing starts in education. And lefties don't wait until university to begin.

SILENCING IN PRIMARY SCHOOLS

Our primary schools are the start of the creeping problem that is hampering right-minded debate in this country. State schools are a rash of liberal thinking, awash with right-on speak and teachers keen to push their own agenda.

Worried parents email me all the time with examples of things that have gone on in their five- or six-year-olds' classrooms that have made them mad.

It is actively taught in UK state schools that Trump is the personification of hate. That he is a bad man.

It is actively taught that any kind of anti-immigration stance is far right and Nazi – no matter the arguments that surround it. There is only one view permitted.

I have examples of small children telling their parents to vote to remain in Europe or their lives will be bad for ever. Of children being sent home after we voted to leave because 'your parents will probably be crying tonight because they will be sad for your future'. Of children given Clinton Mints in advance of the American elections to help persuade them Clinton was the right answer. And being graded higher for explaining why Trump meant the end of civilisation as we know it.

An angry dad emailed me, sick to death of the fact that his son at a nice private school had been shown a clip of me being my usual direct and witty self on the sofa on *This Morning* and had been tasked to write an essay to explain why he disagreed with and hated what I said.

I offered to write it for him.

It is a curious day for education when a child is asked to write an essay about why my views are wrong. Not 'Katie Hopkins is talking nonsense: discuss', or 'Katie Hopkins is an icon of the Conservative right: discuss', but why I am hateful and wrong.

Which I would argue is the opposite of what we should

be trying to teach our kids to do. Don't tell them what to think. They have plenty of influencers in their lives doing that already. Teach them how to think. Make them argue for the opposite thought. Make them assess facts and search left and right for their opinions. And then let them argue a view.

The son was confused. He didn't know whether to write an essay supporting some of my opinions – which were really about the impact of parents on their children, and their future opportunities in life – or do as the teacher ordered, write an essay on how much of an idiot I am, and get an easy high mark.

It's a tough call.

And this lad and his dad aren't alone. I also have an email from a girl who was confused by a school assembly at which Hope Not Hate was given a platform and started mocking right-wingers as Nazis, sneering at Brexiteers, ridiculing Trump supporters and mocking Conservatives as redundant.

Is this really hope for our children?

These are challenging times for students. Children speak about being humiliated at school if they are not leftie liberal in their thought. One mum rang into my radio show in tears because her son had quit his politics class after no one would sit next to him on account of him being a Trump supporter. The teacher's response? She advised him to tone down his views.

And another mum whose kids put their hands up in assembly to say their parents were voting UKIP and had been made to feel humiliated and ashamed by the teacher in front of the whole school.

I have taken hundreds of these letters with me to meet the CEO of Ofsted and his Deputy Dog. His press officer came along for the ride. They would not even have a photo of me in the corridor because they couldn't be seen to be near someone so right-wing.

They had no answers or solutions either. They would not comment on whether any of the examples I showed them were wrong, would not state categorically that teaching Trump-equals-hate is wrong, and would not accept that there was an issue in schools.

The advice they give parents is to complain on a case-by-case basis and request an inspection. And we all know what happens during Ofsted inspections. Teachers pretend to have a plan. Kids are told which questions to ask and primed to ask them, and the really thick ones are given the day off to avoid any disruption. If that isn't gaming the system then I don't know what is.

This is what we are up against.

I am not accepting any of this. As we speak, I should be part way through my Stand Strong School Tour, where I have virtually had to force my way in to state schools to be heard.

TES were horrified and launched a poll: 'Should Katie Hopkins be allowed to speak in schools?' This backfired a bit when 60 per cent of the 20,000 respondents said yes. The Welsh Education Minister joined the fun and said I should not be allowed to talk in schools because I am unkind and unelected. And in Scotland, the Cabinet Minister for Education and Skills started correcting my tweets. Does it make you wonder? Why do the political establishment want to close me down?

Lefties hate it when they are forced to stop listening to their own echo.

SILENCING VIA SOCIAL WORKERS

Some people imagine they can silence me via my kids. They know I am a mum, they know I have three children under twelve and they have reported me to social services over my children. Twice.

The complaints suggest my children are being abused or ill-treated and that they need the help of social services because I am a neglectful mother.

Members of the public can file these complaints anonymously but social services are duty-bound to follow up. I completely understand and respect them for this.

The first gentleman from social services who called and explained why he was calling caught me off guard. I was just about to do a talk to an audience at News International on the South Bank. I had only just got off the phone from my evening call home, in which I speak to each of my children and husband in turn to catch up on the day and feel better about the world. Mark had just bought prawns as a treat and was cooking them for tea. We never have king prawns for tea so I was jealous and happy for them all at the same time.

Then the phone rang and it was social services saying they had received a report and were concerned for the welfare of my kids.

I was shocked. In my head I had a picture of them around the kitchen table, having a nice time – a laugh or a moan about their day, the odd row over something trivial, pleased with themselves that Daddy had done a nice thing and bought them special tea. In my ear I had a polite man from social services asking if I believed my children's welfare was an issue.

And further away in the distance I imagined the deeply malevolent and morally bankrupt individual who thought that reporting me to social services was an acceptable way to air their grievance against my views. That perhaps they could silence me by questioning my love for my children. Their ambition to have me shut down was such that they were prepared to involve social services (who I imagine are busy with important things) to see if they could effect this.

That has happened. Twice.

I wonder what goes through the head of someone, that they can get so angry that I have a voice and they so dislike the things I say that they would attack my family. Have they thought about their end goal, I wonder? What are they hoping for? To have my children taken away? To celebrate a picture of me looking upset as social services invade my home?

Social services tell me all this is pretty standard. They have seen a surge in reports against minor celebrities and outspoken famous faces. The higher the profile, the more reports they get. But their hands are tied because they must follow up.

I admire everything they do, and I can only say lovely things about the people I spoke to, who were kind and sympathetic even though, in effect, I was causing them extra work.

I remember saying to the man, 'But they just had king prawns for tea!' Like that meant anything.

The only thing I wish is that, if a complaint is found to be one that is intended only to harass me for my professional life, the complainant would lose their anonymity. I would like to have the name and address of any individual that reports me as a mother, in order to front up to them as a mother and find out what on earth would motivate them to do such a thing.

My gut says these attacks on my family are made by other women. They understand the thing that would hurt me the most. And they are protected by being female, so they give it a shot.

I say to these women: hate on me? Fine. No problem. I put myself out there so, in my opinion, I need to be able to suck it up. If I don't like it I can sit at home on my sofa and live quietly away from the spotlight as many others sensibly choose to do.

But implying my kids are in danger because of the way they are cared for in the privacy of our home is a pretty low blow by anyone's standards. Please be better than this.

And it's these things, this madness you have to get used to if you are not to be silenced.

SILENCING BY THE POLICE

The police have other reasons for being involved in my silencing. I used to be a massive fan of law and order and still am when it comes to the lads putting themselves in the line of fire to try to keep us relatively safe in uncertain times.

But as individuals progress higher up the career ladder and the chain of command, the less time I have for them. And at the moment, when the line between policing and politicking becomes blurred, they can consider me a right royal pain in the arse.

If they want a story to disappear quietly, I will blast it across the media. If they are hoping to sweep incompetence under the carpet, I will shake that thing in the breeze for the world to see. And if they give their officers impossible conditions to work under (such as the alleged collusion of the West Midlands Police so that local imams could decide who should be allowed to patrol in their area), you can expect an email from one of your officers to end up in my inbox.

It is usually my tweets that get me into trouble. I say this as if it is a pet over which I have no control, like a dog that occasionally bites children and which I must apologise for. I don't mean it that way. I accept full responsibility for my Twitter feed and the pleasure and madness it causes in equal measure.

My newspaper columns also have the ability to land me in a police station answering questions, which is pretty bonkers in an age of free speech and a free press.

After I likened the migrants crossing the Med to cockroaches, due to their sheer tenacity and ability to survive anything, the head of the United Nations Commission on Human Rights singled me out as the biggest threat to world peace on the planet today.

Which is interesting given we are under attack from ISIS, have an obesity epidemic, are beset by financial crises, have a migration disaster pending, have climate change turning us to toast, and Russia and the US are toeing a line similar to that of the Cold War era.

Despite this, Hopkins, sitting at home on her old PC, is enemy number one.

It is always the same. The letter from the police force tasked to head up the complaint arrives on a Friday afternoon around 2 p.m. I am never entirely clear why this is, other than they hope to p*ss on your whole weekend.

I eventually reached an arrangement with my then agent whereby she would keep these letters warning me I was being investigated, or would need to be interviewed at a police station, until Monday. After all, why ruin a good weekend worrying? It achieves nothing. I have the same rule in life: never pass on bad news late at night. Even if someone has died, you aren't going to know about it until the morning because you will be a whole lot more use to everyone if you were given the gift of sleep.

My 'cockroach' column – which has been layered with all sorts of meaning I never intended, such as echoes of the Rwandan genocide and the idea that a race of people are as unimportant as insects – resulted in a protracted investigation, the culmination of which saw me inside Charing Cross police station facing two friendly officers and a tape machine.

In their defence, they looked very apologetic about having me there.

And after I had delivered my four-page rant to them incorporating my own views and the legal substructure brilliantly crafted by my genius lawyer, they went mute and stopped the tape.

Genius lawyer says it is the first time he has seen two police officers look more afraid than the person he was defending. Which is terribly kind, but his genius is the stuff of legend and I love him deeply.

Rather brilliantly for a lawyer, he also looks like a plumber or a chippie. Out of his formal wear, you would think he drove a white van and would be pretty hot on the dance floor. He also looks like Jake Wood, the ginger one from *EastEnders* who was captivating on *Strictly*. Which is great.

This is one of my rules for life: get a lawyer who looks like a bit of a lad, a bit thick. When he turns out to have one of the sharpest legal minds in the UK, you have bagged yourself a winner.

Murdoch has him now. But I know he is watching me quietly from the sidelines.

The investigative team from the homicide and major crime command referred me to the Crown Prosecution Service. They said they were somewhat obliged, because the case was brought by the Society of Black Lawyers, and they had to be seen to be taking them seriously.

But the CPS saw sense, recognised there were no realistic grounds for prosecution success, and turned the case down.

All for one word in one column in a tabloid paper that has its own legal team and editorial guidelines. We live in mad times.

Other police responses have been more for publicity – theirs, not mine – and for the sake of being seen to be doing something, rather than actually doing something more impactful.

I would describe this as abuse of taxpayer funding. But then I am probably biased, what with being a taxpayer and also being the one under investigation for being gobby on Twitter.

Most of the police forces in the south-west were involved in my tweet in which I called certain Palestinians burrowing beneath Israel 'rodents'. Two officers forced themselves into my house under false pretences and told me I had to report to the station for questioning.

But that was resolved once the news gave up on the story.

And the Scottish police force called me in the middle of the night in Australia at Christmas to say they were considering repatriating me to the UK to answer questions about another tweet. I remember sitting up in bed next to Lovely Mark, in Australia, trying to work out why on earth some bloke with a British accent was telling me off and threatening to fly me home.

I had called the nurse who returned to the UK with Ebola an 'ebola bomb' because she had been sent to London for treatment from Scotland. I believe I also used the term 'Sweaty Jocks' instead of 'Sweaty Socks' and that was seen as racist, too.

All in all, it was eleven out of ten on their offence-o-meter scale and the Scottish twitterati were up in arms.

This is how it usually rolls:

I tweet something snappy.

All of Scotland (or at least insert the place or group of people I have offended that day) takes umbrage.

The truly enraged report me to their mums, Twitter and the police.

The police respond on their Twitter feed saying they are investigating and taking these matters very seriously, etc.

The online press picks it up.

I receive a letter on a Friday afternoon after 2 p.m. telling me I am the subject of a serious and vital investigation about

my nasty Twitter feed, and I am guilty of race hate or something else.

It all goes quiet because everyone has been seen to be doing
their job.

SILENCING BY OFCOM

The establishment has other agencies of control, outside of
the police and state organisations.

If you are in the business of live radio, Ofcom is a nightmare. It effectively polices the airways against a list of crimes
and misdemeanours that cannot be spelled out precisely, but
which you are expected to avoid.

Which is kind of like telling your kids to cross the road
with their eyes shut. Or standing against the wall while someone throws knives at your eyes – eventually one is going to
hit the mark.

Some things are obvious. You can't sit on radio and say shit,
fuck or bollocks. Or call someone a wanker. (Though I will
admit I have done that holding the COUGH button.)

You cannot, for example, be overtly offensive, or tell someone to go suck their mum. I applaud all of this. But even on a
talk radio station known for its opinionated content, you are
supposed to give some kind of balance.

You remember that checklist of right and wrong? The
opinions you are supposed to have? Being pro-Palestine and
anti-Israel is right up there on the top of the list. The day I
launched into an all-out rant about why I loved Israel, why I
thought Benjamin Netanyahu was the best thing since sliced
bread, and why his spokesperson at the Israeli embassy, Mark

Regev, was in my top three list of potential future husbands, Ofcom got involved.

This is how it rolls with Ofcom:

I have a massive rant about something I think.

Some utter pillock complains to Ofcom because they don't like my opinion.

Ofcom writes in to my big boss warning him they have launched an investigation and they are taking it extremely seriously.

I get asked to produce some defence for myself, including any balance I have brought in to show there is another side to the debate (bearing in mind this is not the BBC), and I get a meeting with the boss to have my knuckles rapped. And I have to try not to giggle.

In my defence of the pro-Israeli rant, I recalled how I had read out some texts and tweets from people who thought I was a deluded maniac.

But according to transcripts from Ofcom, who obviously pleasure themselves while transcribing entire hours of my radio show, I had prefaced the outstanding 'balance' I had brought into the show with the words: 'According to these texts and tweets from a bunch of quinoa-eating, vegan liberal lefties from Islington…'

Luckily I got off with a warning. But again, the silencing is at work. I rant about my opinions on a talk show where callers are openly invited to come on and give theirs, and somehow this is enough to get me in trouble and under investigation for my views.

And this, my friends, is more of the stuff you have to get used to if you are not going to be silenced by the mob.

People ask me how I handle all the hate and all the unkind things people say online, but they don't even see the half of it.

Someone random person might say they want to rape me with a machete, but then they get bored and sod off. The establishment is far more sinister. And the tentacles of its institutions and organisations are much more intimidating.

Unlucky for them, I am not easily frightened. Against all this, I stand strong.

And in the face of all this, I continue to fight to have my voice heard.

I tell people I really mean what I say. When you see what I am up against, I need to have the courage of my convictions locked and loaded at my side to keep me standing strong.

CHAPTER 8

AVOID. AVOID
~~SNOG~~. ~~MARRY~~. AVOID.

Sometimes I wonder if I am the only one who sees it. You know? The annoying stuff of every day that makes you want to throw up your arms and bark, 'Were you born an idiot or do you have to practise?'

When people are too stupid to know what they should do, or when they know what they should do but don't do it, then we step in as a country and help them along a bit. Help them do the opposite of what they should be doing.

Parent and child parking spaces are a good example. You can argue as much as you like that they are close to the supermarket for the safety of the children, but I don't buy that argument.

New mums are generally overweight women. And overweight women need to walk. If I were in charge, parent and child spaces would be at the farthest reaches of the car park, in the back corner where the dodgy white camper van has been parked for close to three months.

That way, the kids are out of harm's reach, and the mother gets a good stroll on before she even gets as far as the frozen chicken nuggets.

The people who park in parent and child spaces are pretty much the same people who park right next to the door of the gym. They know what the sensible answer is, or what they should do (like walk, or do more exercise) but given the option will always make the wrong choice or take the easy way out.

A perfect example of this easy way out is the lazy parenting that is pandemic in the state school system.

When you rock up to dispatch your precious little four-year-old into class, hoping he is about to enter a lifetime of learning, frankly you haven't got a hope in hell. You just spent four years teaching your baby to eat nicely, training him to pee in the toilet instead of casually on the floor, getting him to share nicely with your mates' kids, and making sure his face is washed and hair brushed before you start each day.

He says 'thank you' on command and knows it is not worth crying for nothing because you aren't that much of a schmuck. And you have more pressing things to get on with than dealing with a yelling person.

And there you stand. Outside the classroom on day one. Looking around at the other kids. Looking at some of the mothers of the other kids. And you know all hope is lost.

Here are a few of the children to identify early.

THE BITING KID

There is always one. Minimum. They are standard issue at a state school and spend the entire day acting like a crocodile in an acid swamp trying to bite your kid. Biting kid belongs to the mother in pyjamas, the one still angry that she has to get out of bed for something so trivial as school. The mum who never associated the excitement and attention of pregnancy with ten years of 7 a.m. starts and 3 p.m. pick-ups, but rather with the excitement of buying a stroller and having somewhere to hang her Primark shopping bags when slopping around the town centre in leggings and a pool slide.

THE KID WITH THE BULGING SHORTS

The kid with the bulging shorts is in pull-ups because his mother couldn't be arsed to put in the tedious hours sitting in the bathroom on her knees reading books or making strange noises supposed to encourage her child to do a wee. You have to ask yourself, if the kid is still doubly incontinent, and his mother (there will be no father) has been unable to teach him the things we are able to teach cats or hamsters, how much of the alphabet is she likely to have conveyed? Assuming she even knows the alphabet and, take it from me, that is not a given.

In the *Big Brother* house with Alicia Douvall (she of the multiple plastic surgeries and rock-hard boobs), I nearly fell off my kitchen stool when she said she was home-schooling her kid and had only learned the alphabet earlier that year. She was thirty-six. I can virtually guarantee you that a kid who cannot wee in the toilet will not know the difference between a curly C and a kicking K.

THE DODGY-SMELLING KID

One of the parents will be a staunch environmentalist, more vegan than an actual cabbage, whose biggest achievement in life will be that her total household waste each week can fit into the shell of an egg. Which will also be recycled. Enviro-mum cares more about saving water than using it for the purposes for which it was intended. Like washing. Hence the kid glancing past your clean child on their way to class, smelling a bit like damp dog, with hair unwashed since his birth, who will be responsible for the outbreak of worms you will endure towards week three of term.

THE IDIOT

This can be tougher. It does not follow that the thick mum anxious to get back to repeats of Jeremy Kyle will actually have the thickest kid; being exceptionally stupid is a gift bestowed quite at random. But one thing is for sure: if your kid is vaguely equipped for school and well behaved, in that they don't spit, bite or piss their way through class, they will get lumbered with the class idiot, whose only route to attention is the childhood equivalent of self-pleasuring in a public car park.

Your child, in whom you have invested four years of effort, will become the idiot's babysitter. Because they are good, they are paired with the idiot in order to take some of the burden off the teacher. It's a position your child never asked for or wanted.

If you ask your child 'who did you sit next to today?' and find the answer is always 'Brandon', you will have found the class idiot.

While your well-behaved kid has been obliged to fulfil the role of teacher's wingman, one other child in class will have been awarded the title of 'special assistant'.

The teacher's special assistant is the learning equivalent of anthrax, a kid with more issues than Denise Welch. Our 'special assistant' was promoted to the role after deciding not to throw the brick in his hand through the window.

Instead of fast-tracking these kids to the penitentiary system, where they will always end up, they are given special privileges such as extra Golden Time for anything they were planning to do wrong but didn't. Less stick and carrot, more endless enthusiasm and Xbox.

THE GIFTED KID

I am never sure which is the bigger curse, being stupid or being monumentally gifted. I suspect there is a higher prevalence of suicide among the latter, as well as a far lower incidence of sexual relations, much less marriage. Which is a pity.

The gifted child will be reading *The Hobbit* as they wait to be let into the classroom, be crap at all sports, be short, and already have a twitch and squint of epic proportions.

I look at these kids and, to save myself from shedding actual tears of sorrow, I remember there is a place in this world for all of us, and someone has to be an accountant. Or want to work in the transport division of the local council offices. Or study astronomy. You should try to encourage your own kid to embrace the gifted kid with parenting phrases like 'it's good to be odd' and 'the world's greatest leaders were social outcasts' while showing them pictures of Elon Musk, Bill Gates or the fabulous Steve Jobs, who was rejected by his own mother at birth.

I also know from experience that being the weird kid can

come with benefits. You are never going to fit in with the cool crowd, so you don't need all that complex approval. You only need one other weird kid and you are mates for life.

THE HOME-SCHOOL KID

There will always be a kid destined to be withdrawn from state school by the age of eight to be home-schooled. You can pick them out very easily: they usually have a frumpy mum who is wildly devoted to Radio 4, has an innate distrust of everything, sees the world as a huge contaminating agent, and carries miniature bottles of antibacterial handwash in her bag.

Held in high suspicion by all normal mums, home-school mum is planning to remove her precious kids from all human contact and spend her every waking moment in their company. She chants 'mum knows best' like a mantra at breakfast. She regards hairdressers and Tampax as extreme violations of her family's privacy. Her poor kids are so sheltered their skin is virtually translucent; they're the ones you'll see dressed head to toe in sun suits from late March onwards.

Home-school kids tend to end up at real school at some point, terrified and wide eyed, where they will be beaten up for calling 'Miss' 'Mummy', and will repeatedly have to hide in the toilets from Brandon, who wants to cut off their absurdly long hair.

My advice: any mother who wants to closet her kids away at home when most normal children are nicking each other's packed lunches and building dens is certifiable. Run.

This is the company you will be in when you stand outside

the door of the classroom, waiting to hand over the kid you really tried your best with, the kid you are proud of, the kid about to be exposed to elements of society you never even imagined. All you can do is hope they will survive.

And this carries on through life. You can suss out the same patterns at work as at school, the same types of people and the same ways of thinking and operating. Adults are just the same as kids and the office is no different to the classroom.

Which is why the office fridge is always such a virulent breeding ground for hatred: people are basically animals and we are not designed to be in such close proximity with one another.

People will nick your milk, steal your Cadburys Creme Egg, sneak some of your cordial and swipe an entire sandwich pack if they think they can get away with it.

If you are thinking of taking up the offer of a new job, ask to see the office fridge first. At one glance you will know exactly what you are dealing with.

If there is food padlocked to the shelf, more post-it notes than an HR workshop, or a regular pint of milk labelled 'breast milk', remember that these people will be your colleagues. Signs like 'I have licked this sandwich' show the lengths people have to go to survive.

The class idiot will now be in HR. Having failed to find an actual purpose or achieve anything other than a dodgy 2:1 in social sciences from a former polytechnic, Sheila has worked out her special gift in life and the thing she likes best is… gossiping.

HR is perfect for this. And she will be able to channel her

special gossiping skills to full effect while conducting useless training days on the sort of crap you really don't need to know. Training days entitled 'Team work and co-operation', involving endless flip charts and post-it notes, despite it being perfectly clear that Sheila would shaft you with a single email if she could achieve the necessary collateral to do so.

By now the gifted kid in class with the tragic squint and slightly inward-pointing feet will have gone one of two ways. Life will have either embraced their unique qualities or bullied said qualities out of them. This will have forced them towards the church, chemsex or an uncertain life on the streets. Or they might have found their niche. A niche that usually involves communicating by code with other tech nerds who prefer equipment to actual people because tech is far safer than random human emotions.

The Google building in London is a perfect example of the natural habitat of the geek. It makes me feel like a naked boy in a segregated unit for paedo priests: vulnerable. The lifts have no buttons on the inside, leaving you to wonder where you were trying to get to, where you are going and how you will know if you have got there – all while you try to out-cool some kid in trainers who is clearly going to be master of the universe one day.

Despite hating human contact, geeks love shared space. Every space is shared and every bit of it is as uncomfortable as they can possibly make it. A chair must be a pouffe. A table must stand at a quirky angle. A telephone must look like a vibrator and be impossible to use as an actual tool for communication.

This is hostile terrain for a regular human like my good self, but heaven for the geek.

I have found in adult life, just as in school life and at Geek HQ, that there are types of people you don't want to be, people to avoid at all costs, even if your mother taught you to try to be nice to everyone.

1. SHORT MEN

Nothing good ever came from a short man except more short men. As keeper of the foof of power and custodian of the embryo of hope, you are also queen of the next generation. Your job is to ensure this does not include more short men.

Short men have two ways in which to compensate. Well, three actually, although the third involves being exceptionally well hung, which is a blessing bestowed by the gods in return for the genetic twist of misfortune that halted growth at five foot two.

The strange thing about a well-hung dwarf is that everything looks longer if your legs are shorter. My husband has a bit of this. He is nearly six foot but his legs are only thirty inches long. I maintain this is why his member reaches halfway to his knee.

I guess the only way to fact-check a man's member is with your own vaginal scanner. If size is relative to leg length, then at least your foof is a constant in this mathematical conundrum.

I digress.

Members dressed to one side, short men have two options. They can either be really funny or really wide.

Funny is good. I remember a guy around town when I was growing up who was only about five foot but hugely popular. Tony May. I remember him as cute, funny and often found clinging to the ample bosoms of my posh mate, Hannah Ford.

I didn't think of him as short then, and don't remember him as short now. But he definitely was.

I am certain he will have gone on to be exactly the same into adulthood. He's probably a great dad by now, too.

(If it turns out he struggled with depression, lost a winning lottery ticket and topped himself playing blue whale on t'internet, I apologise to his family in advance.)

Ladies, as custodians of the embryo of hope, you can make exceptions for the funny ones. The rules are not hard and fast. We can be flexible.

But going wide is a terrible idea. As soon as you see bulging neck muscles and biceps on a bloke in an overly tight top, you know you are dealing with **short** in bold. SHORT in caps lock. Short on road rage. This man is shouting: YES I AM FUCKING SHORT AND YES I AM REALLY PISSED OFF ABOUT IT SO I GO TO THE GYM. PUSHING WEIGHTS IS MY BODY'S WAY OF CRYING.

There is such a thing as over-compensation and short men don't seem to realise we can see it a mile off. Worse still, they only put in the effort in the neck and arm department, leaving their legs to look rather chicken-like.

It's the short, male, body-building equivalent of me only shaving up to my knees, leaving a dense thicket of hair from the thigh up.

To add to the effect, they usually go for a few tattoos as

well. This is a bit like those nasty-bastard fish that live just under the sand and have long, venomous prickles they shove up into your foot when you stand on them.

Or snails. Or hedgehogs. Or porcupines.

Basically, the smaller you are, the weirder the armour you put on to make up for the fact that you might be overlooked in life.

Porcupines have prickles. Short men have biceps and tattoos.

2. GINGER PEOPLE

When my son was born I had only two wishes: that he would have my legs, and that he would not be ginger. The ginger affliction is well known but not spoken about now, as ginger-shaming verges on racism or bullying.

I'm just putting it out there, but the largest sperm bank in Norway stopped accepting donations from ginger people due to a lack of demand. The free market has no shame.

And all mothers know the one thing you don't want is a ginger baby. The first words out of my mouth after Max exited my vagina with a pop were, 'Is he ginger?'

And you can say I am a cow all you like. I have had this exact conversation with so many women, I know it is not just me.

There is a way to check whether your man has ginger genes. My advice to you, ladies, is to get the potential father of your children to grow a beard. You may be happily married to a man you think is more brunette than Eva Longoria, but I tell you this: if there is a ginger gene, it always shows itself in the beard. I thought Mark was a pure-bred brunette. Then the beard came and there was a fleck of red. Imagine my horror.

I did tweet once, 'Ginger babies. Just like regular babies. Only so much harder to love.'

Which admittedly was a bit harsh and means mothers of red-headed kids always give me the evil eye.

But the true orange-ginger is quite something, and tends to go hand in hand with people I don't like – such as Nicola Sturgeon, the Ginger Dwarf from the North. Not only one of my least favourite people on the planet, but also incredibly ginger. And short. Which leads me to believe my theory on people you don't want to meet is pretty sound.

There are ginger pride days, I think. And periodically magazines run pictures of beautiful ginger models looking ... beautiful. Which is all very well, but if you snapped the average overweight ginger shopper in the high street in cheap leggings and a pink anorak, the picture would not be quite so pretty.

Either way, I am glad I am not ginger and nor are my kids. Life is hard enough already without adding to the challenges. (This probably counts as hate speech and I will be reported by the Met Police's online hate squad as soon as this goes to print. I stand braced for their letter, which I look forward to receiving at 2 p.m. on a Friday afternoon.)

3. FUSSY EATERS

Environmentalists go hand in hand with the gluten-free brigade. I often wonder which came first: being self-centred or being gluten-free. It's the ultimate badge of the narcissist – needing to shape the world around you because you are so truly special.

And if you can't be special because of the things you have achieved, be special by giving yourself an affliction. Be lactose intolerant or gluten sensitive.

When mothers tell me their kid is gluten-free, I politely explain my kid's party isn't, so they are the one with choices to make, not me.

I know a mother who made her kid's party totally gluten-free just because her kid was. This screams: 'I am miserable – so I am going to make everyone else miserable as well.'

4. ECO-FREAKS

You know very well that eco-mum is never happy unless you can see just how eco she is. She cycles to school with her unwashed children clinging to the frame of her bike, helmet stuck to her egg-white-washed hair.

Usually called Pippa or Meredith, eco-mums up-cycle school uniforms from tablecloths and home-craft shoes from strands of willow. They are invariably late, partly because they read *The Guardian* and are asserting their right to independence, but mainly because they have been recycling uneaten cornflakes on top of the boiler.

My advice: feel pity for the kids. Their diet is raw vegan and they are usually lumbered with names like 'Otis' or 'Oscar'. Sneak them a crafty burger whenever you get the chance.

Inevitably, a lot of this is about mums. Because when you look at a kid, you are really looking at the mother. And I say that in the knowledge that I will probably pick my middle child up from the police station before she is sixteen. My father says my middle child is my punishment for me being me. And finds it hilarious.

I've always said that behind every fat kid is a fat mother, and I still think this is completely true. The school playground proves it. Most mums leg it in, throw their kids at the classroom, shout instructions to be good, and leg it out again.

Fat mum lurks outside in her Citroen Picasso. She does drop-off and pick-up without ever actually leaving the car. She glowers at the lollipop man, smashes over the pavement outside the gate, and belches out her fat kids in a cloud of cigarette smoke and crisp packets. Fat mum is sometimes replaced by fat dad. They look similar except the dad supports Arsenal.

When handling these types I advise you to stare open-mouthed at their sheer size. Especially if they are wearing lycra.

Worse still is the Parent Teachers Association mum.

Having given up a job she loved for her kids, PTA mum has found her calling as head of the Parent Teacher Association. She volunteers for every awful school trip going and has her CRB clearance taped to her forehead at all times. By virtue of having raised a 'staggering' £34.52 last year, through the endless graft of dozens of exhausted mums over 2,500 hours, she sees herself as a sort of Melinda Gates – forever giving. Smug doesn't even come close.

My advice: avoid at all costs. PTA mum is endlessly scouting for volunteers. Before you know it, she will sign you up to run the bouncy castle at the school fete and teach the goons in Key Stage 1 how to sew.

There is also dad-mum.

I always thought the curious incident of the dad in the

playground was blooming odd, and would look at him and feel only pity.

Invariably short and beardy, dad-mum usually works in a supremely dull public-sector job, probably in the transport division. Imagining sex with dad-mum makes me gag in my mouth.

My advice: the dad-mum is to be avoided at all costs in case he tries to join you for coffee.

I know mums who recall their playground-duty years as being filled with abject fear and dread. They hated doing it, hated the other mums, and hated all the cosy groups in the playground looking down on those of us who didn't want to be part of all that.

I once tried to join in and was invited for coffee after the school run. By the time it was all over, it was nearly time for another school run. I think this is how these women fill their days. And they are fulfilled by it, which I still find utterly odd.

People say it is wrong to judge people this way. To make an instant assessment of someone based on the way they look, walk, drive or act with their kids. I don't think it's wrong. I love watching people, making guesses about their lives, digging to see if I can get to their truth.

And it's a good skill to have.

For example, I know that the photographer who took the picture of little Alan Kurdi on the beach was a woman. I've never looked it up to check, but I know. It's the feet. Mothers have a special connection with children's feet, especially the soles of their feet.

One of the most amazing things about your new baby is

their little feet and little tiny toes. If you are lucky and have a
baby shaped like it is supposed to be, their littlest toes will be
so tiny that you could cut the whole damn thing off trying to
trim their toenails.

I nearly did just that with my first baby, and went out the
same day and bought the little clippers you are supposed to
have instead.

There is a reason you love sitting playing with their feet, strok-
ing the soft little undersole which has never touched a floor, its
skin so pure it could make you weep. And a reason my daughter's first pair of shoes is still on her bed stand. A reason mums
make moulds of their babies' feet to keep, a way of remembering
how tiny they were before they grew up and went away.

That photographer focused on the soles of the child's feet.
Because they were so tiny, so perfect. The photographer was
a woman.

Sadly, so is the idiot chancellor of the University of Hull.

Hull University announced that any student who failed to
be gender sensitive in their essays would be marked down.
So no more he or she. Out goes workmanship and tradesman
and in comes they, s/he and tradesperson.

No disrespect to Hull, but the last thing a student needs to
be worrying about when writing essays is gender sensitivity.
How exactly does that work with *The Taming of the Shrew*? Or
Romeo and Juliet – is Romeo a 'they'; is Juliet?

More importantly, do we need a new generation of individuals programmed to believe we are all gender fluid? That
no one has a gender to call their own? That we are all, in fact,
they? Because I believe that is a load of tosh.

And, more importantly, the students need to decide whether or not that is a load of tosh. Not the authorities.

Skilled as I am at making instant assumptions, I know, just by reading about the lunacy being imposed at the Hull asylum, that the boss is a woman. And sure enough, I go to Google and there she is: Virginia Bottomley, the UK's first female chancellor of a university.

Doesn't that tell you everything you need to know? She is clearly desperate, lonely and has cats. And believes the best way she can make a name for herself is to impose a nonsensical ruling that feels like it reflect woman's ability to promote tolerance and integration.

Women like this are such an embarrassment.

Instead of coming to the job and making a vital impact, outperforming the record of the last chancellor, or taking Hull to a new level of performance, the best thing she can do is implement a rule which requires no competitive effort.

It does not test her authority or decision-making, does not set out her stand and challenge others to beat her, does not make her a commercial thinker. It makes her a woman. Defined by her gender with the very rule she imposed about gender sensitivity.

I don't know if that is irony or stupidity. Or just plain sad. I fear it may be the latter.

Getting the measure of people quickly is crucial in an interview which may only last for four minutes and will be broadcast live around the world.

If you can quickly assess your opponent's stance, identify some weakness while you are still in the makeup room, by the time you get in front of the camera you will have all the ammunition you need to be a success.

I think this is really at the heart of my journey from business to media. On *The Apprentice*, the tasks and team leadership roles were easy for me. I won every task I led.

What got me ahead was being able to understand the weaknesses of the characters I was set against, and being able to expose them in a pithy way to the camera. And I simply refused to be shamed or apologise for being blunt.

I assumed, of course, that everyone else was being equally frank. I assumed wrong.

I didn't know it at the time, but being able to dismiss one woman as an orange idiot and describing another as being best friends with Mr Pinot and Mr Grigio, and being pretty handy in an argument turned out to be the keys to a whole new career.

CHAPTER 9

BEWARE THE BIG-BOOBERS

Think of all the really dangerous things in life – ebola, terror, Cillit Bang in your eyeball, your mother-in-law when she feels left out – and you're probably going to overlook one massive group of subversives who are possibly the most dangerous and powerful of all.

They are moving among us, hiding in plain sight. They are incognito, highly camouflaged, resilient and trained by experts in their field. And they are unstoppable.

They are women over forty. And at just forty-two, I am one of them.

Yes, I know, I know, I look about sixty. If I'm forty-two, you're Myra Hindley, you thought I was ninety-five … I have heard it all before.

My age has been something of an issue all my life. At eighteen, people thought I was twenty. At twenty-eight – *The Apprentice* years – people guessed around thirty-five, and now, at forty-two, people think I am over fifty. The other day someone told me their grandma was in better shape than me.

Thanks to various social media and internet forums, I have ended up with two official birthdays – like the Queen, but remarkably less privileged. My age has become such a thing that people think I am one of those weird people in the media who does not want their real age known so they can pretend to be twenty-five for ever.

Nancy Dell'Olio is a fine example, last seen with more plastic in her face than is floating about the Atlantic Ocean. I feel sorry for the love. She has gone the full Mickey Rourke.

Or Carol Vorderman, who is brilliant and brave but has chosen to turn her face into a pillow full of nonsense instead.

Others say that being full of hate takes its toll on your face and that's why I look like a melted wheelie bin or a slapped arse. Or have 'more wrinkles than my ball sack', to quote a reliable source.

Either way, women over forty are largely invisible in public life.

Aside from the childless few who have risen to the top of politics, like Merkel, May and Sturgeon, thanks to having too much spare time on their hands and being able to function unhindered by guilt or the school run, or unchallenged by thoughts of whether there is more to life than pretending to be in charge of stuff – apart from them, there is a dearth of us older broads with babies and a sex life in the higher ranks of media, politics and industry.

Contrary to the verging-on-psychopathic whinging of the feminists, who are pretty sure someone else is always to blame for everything (especially if that person has a penis), there are two simple facts that explain this absence of women.

For starters, most have of us have got more sense. We choose happiness over professional kudos, and the company of our family over the fawning of colleagues paid to do so. Once we earn over a certain amount of money, more doesn't make sense. The stuff you have to give up to achieve it just isn't worth the extra amount you would take home. No matter how many zeros are attached.

It's not that we don't like nice things. Or think we deserve to be paid more. It's just that when we work out how to be happy with what we have, we get really good at it, and fast.

Happiness might be a new top from Primark. It might be a bucket of wine with your mate in All Bar One, or fish and chips on a bench at the beach.

I think we judge our happiness against our own personal index. Less comparing with others as a benchmark, more looking at our best day, best photo or best memory and trying to make that happen again.

Many men spend their days fellating those higher up the greasy pole than themselves in the hope of a bigger bonus. Some do it just to be able to brag that they have stared upward to the heavens of the twenty-eighth floor and seen their boss's anus, gleaming like Saturn above them. Other still dream of a corner office and a view they believe they were born to enjoy.

Many realise they are never going to make it in the fiercely competitive private sector, where competition is, indeed, everything, so they move sideways in order to move up.

These are the worst specimens of all, the public-sector managers who have earned more than they should ever be entitled to in the private sector, and are now scoring six-figure salaries in the National Health Service, leading initiatives with names like 'The Change and Performance Drive' – despite invariably being four stone overweight and slower-moving than your average iceberg.

I bump into these people fairly regularly on the train to London, always seated in first class. The fact that the taxpayers rammed in standard are paying for them to sit in relative splendour really grinds my gears.

One bunch of 'Customer Service Leaders' from the train company itself, lounging in first class, so frustrated my sense of justice that I descended on them, asserting that if they truly wanted to assess the customer experience they would be back in standard trying to fight their way to piss in a dirty bathroom while trying not to touch any given surface for fear of contracting hepatitis C.

Women have also figured out there is only so much in life you can actually control. Once you work out that beyond a certain point health, wealth and longevity can be violently impacted by arbitrary factors outside of our control – like cancer, car crashes, the consumer price index or the cleanliness of the ward where you had your elective surgery – then you decide to focus instead on the one thing you are truly master of: yourself.

The path to this divergence between women and men is well trodden.

Despite the sulphuric acid gushed from the angry mouths of feminists, the statistics back up the fact that women are more equal to men than ever before.

Women are firing along, outperforming boys at school,

hitting university in greater numbers, being promoted faster than boys and getting paid better than them, too.

There is a vast catalogue of evidence to support the assertion that young women are more likely to get the job, to rise up in the job, and to be on the trajectory to the top jobs ahead of the boys across most industries females care to entertain.

Until their first maternity leave. Childbirth is the reason there is perceived inequality in the workplace.

And it is not that employers are malevolent bastards, the equivalent of Herod marauding about demanding all infants be drowned or shot or at least floated down the river in a wicker basket.

Although, as an employer, I can tell you I loathe maternity leave more than I loathe a fat person in a disability car. As a small business employer, paying for someone to have their child is only a short hop away from paying for someone to have sex. And last time I looked, prostitution was illegal.

But out in the real world, women take a long hard look at their life and what is important for their baby, and kowtowing to corporate life just doesn't cut it.

Women want something better for themselves and their babies.

Better than the rat race, better than conniving colleagues, better than their fellow commuters who refuse to stand for them on the Underground.

Maternity leave and the associated hoopla around it takes women to the point of wondering whether it is really all worth it. The haggling for time off, profuse apologising for not being around, watching them recruit someone to replace you who clearly wants your job full time – all combined with the faff of lugging your boobs and belly about while trying to look office-smart. It really makes you question it all.

I distinctly remember working well into my ninth month with India and wearing a rather natty red maternity sweater to the conference I was supposed to be running.

All day I wondered why so many people were staring at my massive bazookas, eventually concluding that American men have a thing for maternal chests.

In fact, my cottonwool nipple pads had slipped. Pregnant women are obliged to wear these to absorb the milk that starts squirting out the minute you even think about the baby you are going to have, and mine had gone south.

All the milk gushing from my nipples had stained my sweater a deep plum. Two dark, blood-coloured spheres of ooze focused the attention like headlights on a crippled kangaroo. I had spent the day startling men with the sight of them.

Maternity leave is actually a royal pain in the arse. I think women would be far better off taking a cash sum from their employers as a farewell gift and starting again at whatever they fancied when they were ready.

Trying to work out when you are leaving and when you are coming back, for what hours and to what job, is just a massive unknown in a sea of uncertainty when you are about to have a child.

With my first pregnancy I avoided maternity leave like the plague, mainly because I was unsure of what I would have done with it. I loved work, loved being on the road with the lads at the managing consultancy I worked for, and loved my life between London and New York. I didn't want to miss a minute of it. You could say – in fact, I would say – I was not ready for children.

I still remember the exact moment I stopped for a second to look in the mirror after taking a shower in my apartment in New York, and had to do a double-take.

I looked different.

I never stopped to look in mirrors. And still don't, really. They remain pretty functional items in my mind. There to check you have vaguely got everything where it is supposed to be and there is no toothpaste on your chin or dinner on your nose.

I still remember looking at my strange, thickened waist and bigger boobs, connecting with the fact I hadn't noticed a period in a good few weeks, and feeling sick at the thought that I needed to take a pregnancy test and I knew what it was going to say.

I wasn't ready for any of the baby stuff. And I certainly wasn't going to spend nine months preparing for it, wafting around maternity and baby shops touching up soft stuff like I do now. I carried on as normal and pretended it wasn't going to happen.

They say denial is one of the stages of grief. I am not certain it is a helpful approach to dealing with a positive pregnancy test and do not recommend it as a course of action.

I can remember lying, direct to the faces of the BA and AA staff at check-in, that I was only five months pregnant but having twins, when actually I was nine months pregnant and about to drop. Just to keep on working.

Other people are more pragmatic. Some yearn for a child, and the moment they become pregnant embark on a glorious journey of puffing out their tummies and buying baby things to max out on the moment.

Don't even get me started on the pin badges. I completely understand that some people are excited to be pregnant. I'd quite like another child myself and if you can pull off a fabulous pregnancy where you are fit and full of beans, it is a glorious time. So much so that newbies want to get to that moment where they are visibly pregnant.

In the interim, instead of waiting secure in the knowledge that their moment will surely come, they decide to wear a bloody badge.

I know they are provided by Transport for London. I appreciate the agreed line that they are designed to help pregnant women get a seat. And to spare the embarrassment of people who stand to give their seat to chubsters who aren't pregnant at all. But a badge? Really?

We all know that what these badges are really for is to let people know you are excited to be pregnant and you are special. You haven't got a bump yet, but you want one, and in the interim you want everyone to know about it.

Sure. But take it from Aunty Hopkins. You have ten months to feel special (the nine-month thing is a lie and a massive conspiracy). By the end of this time you will be on your knees in tears in front of your doctor, begging him to get this thing out of you because it feels like someone is resting a wardrobe on the top of your vagina from the inside.

Make the most of still being slim and active and get

over yourself. You are fertile and you had sex. This is not award-winning stuff.

There is a bit of a tendency for women to make pregnancy and especially childbirth a bit of a serial drama. Like *East-Enders*. It is actually a basic biological function and most animal species push out a baby and crack straight on without needing a medal or a badge.

Take giraffes. They drop their baby out their lady giraffe bits (giraffe-foof, as I like to call it) without so much as a backward glance. Round and round goes her jaw, still chewing on a bit of a high branch as a massive object drops to earth with the equivalent of four full-size wooden crutches attached to its weirdly shaped giraffe body. And she doesn't even flinch.

Whales are pretty awesome mums, too. Out pops baby whale while she's there doing the breast stroke 40,000 leagues under the chilly sea. She barely breaks a stroke and suddenly there are two of them swimming along where there used to be one.

And penguins are the most epic of all mums. They plop out a couple of eggs and hand them over to dad to balance on his feet. He then freezes his bollocks off in the snow while she trots off somewhere altogether more fishy to get a bite to eat.

Penguins have got maternity nailed.

As have seahorses, who are, in fact, the ultimate feminists. They take their eggs and hand them over to the seahorse dad to fertilise, then go off to do more important things like wafting about looking awesome.

Seahorses are rather like the posh mums of Chelsea and Kensington, who leave childbirth too late, hand their eggs over to the poshest private IVF clinic they can find, then swan about looking glamorous and having coffee while someone fertilises the eggs and then hands them over to the au pair when fully formed.

Anyway, back to us normal women. Despite the fact that animals (and some human mums) have got it all worked out, maternity can be a traumatic thing, whether you deny it, take it, dine out on it, or spend the whole of it dry heaving into a toilet bowl swearing you will never have sex again.

All this, and that's before a little gurgling thing comes along with big black eyes and teeny tiny fingers and changes everything you thought you knew, redefining what matters and what really isn't important. And transforming your life such that something as simple as trying to shower and get out of the house feels like running the London Marathon in reverse.

I remember once arriving at work and looking down to find I had two odd shoes on my feet, and wondering whether, in fact, this whole working mum thing was going to work out for me.

After children, women realise they can find and, indeed, should search for fulfilment and validation in something a lot more meaningful than a bunch of boys in cheap suits playing 'who's got the biggest cock' via their pay packets and the staff triathlon.

During my brief tenure in the halls of Barclays in Canary Wharf, I distinctly recall a boardroom full of men comparing shooting rifles and one being declared the winner because he had also managed to screw the lady who flogged them to him.

Aside from being able to understand that a sense of true

fulfilment comes from somewhere other than an office, the second reason women over forty are invisible in public life is that they can achieve far more without the glare of publicity or the kudos of being a known name or face. I say this as a woman with one of the most recognisable noses in the business.

There is a vast army of forty-something women getting on with their lives at work and home who simply don't need the applause of a large crowd to be happy.

My lovely cleaning lady Sarah, who kindly comes to my house for a couple of hours a week to keep my ironing basket vaguely under control and my family from getting sepsis due to unhygienic conditions, is a perfect example of a powerful woman over forty.

She doesn't know it, of course, because she is the loveliest person on the planet and wouldn't say boo to a goose. But she has her lovely husband and is a great sister to a poorly brother and a lovely mum to her grown daughters who still rely on her for advice, support and a multitude of other things.

She does cleaning and housework for people because it suits how she wants to run her life. And if people piss her off more than they should be expected to, she doesn't work for them any more. She is in control of her world. And her world is good. She is a powerful woman. But she doesn't feel the need to shout about it.

So too my lovely friend Lucy, whom I adore more than life itself, mainly because she has double GGs and lets me lie on them or jiggle them if I am lucky.

Again, she has her husband and her two beautiful children

– and they are blooming good looking as well; one models kids clothes, she is that cute.

While her husband gets on with his job being a smart accountant, she provides childcare for other mums and dads so they can drop off early and get to work and pick up late without being trapped by the school run.

The kids are all dropped off with her at 7.30 a.m. She gives them breakfast, gets them shipshape and all set for school, then walks them all to class in a happy crowd of little people. And then she is there again at the end of the school day to collect all eight children, walk them home, sort them out, and give them a home-cooked tea before their parents come to pick them up at 7.30 p.m.

Any of you who has ever done a school run will know just how magnificent a feat this truly is. Picking up one child can involve finding three bags, some homework, a missing blazer, and potentially an informal chat with a teacher about some bad behaviour or other.

How brilliant is she? And how many of you reading this are wishing you had a Lucy in your life?

Bear in mind she does all this with two children of her own to look after and all the dramas and goings-on that can take place between home and school – and she still looks super-smart and snappy doing it. That's an understatement, actually. She looks hot. Properly hot. She looks like she breathes mountain air and drinks only pure spring water, straight from the source. She oozes the sort of fresh-faced, vitamin-based glow we all dream of.

Most school-gate mums look like they have been smoking

weed half the night and have barely managed to get out of their pyjamas or actually find shoes to do the school run.

At this point I need to get a small issue off my chest. I would like it noted for the parenting record that Uggs are not actually shoes. They are slippers worn in the street. I say to any school mum doing the run in Uggs: we both know you haven't had a shower this morning. The best you have had is a quick smear with a wet wipe. Which makes you a wretch.

Lucy and Sarah are the opposite of this, and just two of the vast army of working mums cracking on with their lives, making things work, and putting the total happiness of their family, the sum of their collective happiness, before personal reward or individual gratification.

They are on Facebook to see what their mates are up to and to stay in touch. Not on LinkedIn competing to see who's got the best connections in the job market. And their free time is spent doing the things they love with the people they like best, not being obliged to show their face at some bloody awful networking event.

I love having them as part of my life, and love keeping the people who have helped keep Team Hopkins on the road in my life, too.

My first nanny still works with us thirteen years after she started. She has come and gone – needed more hours or less, found work with others and been in demand. But we have always stayed in touch and now she is back with us two days a week with a son of her own and another one on the way. Full circle and back round again.

Her son is by far the best behaved and cutest child on the

planet and spends his life roaring like a dinosaur or laughing his head off because he can. I love having him around.

It is funny that the lady who spent so much time looking after my girls now looks after one of her own, occasionally in my kitchen. And because she's a pro-mum, he is possibly the best behaved child I know.

Talking of children, I have worked, and still work, with some of the biggest egos in the media business. Typically, they are not the faces you see on your screen. They are the puppeteers who manipulate the celebrity faces and voices: the editors, the series producers, the heads of channel. And their egos are monstrous. Truly.

I know of a newspaper office in which every single professional and highly paid woman wears heels because the editor likes it that way. He believes women in brogues are lesbians.

I rocked up to our first lunch in flats and my new boss apologised for not warning me. As if that would have changed what was on the end of my legs.

I was the only front-facing female at the radio station I worked at for longer than I care to remember, and the male-ness of it all was asphyxiating. White boys employing white men and a website run by a white male who could not recognise that only white non-females featured on the site.

When I was fired, I asked in my polite thank-you note to be replaced by a female. And for my female producer to get a bonus for all her hard work.

Neither of those two things happened. Nor did I expect them to. But at least banging the boys over the head with a frying pan makes them open their eyes and see what's hitting them.

The bosses only have to look at the ratings (higher than 5 live) and clip hit-rates ('most watched clip since launch') to see that boys aren't better. They are just more prepared to get their elbows out, whip their tiny chipolata cocks on the table and demand stuff. And be surrounded by other boys doing the same. Making it a pretty hostile environment for a regular woman.

Women realise faster that life is about much more than all this noise and nonsense. And women over forty know even better. I'd argue we are better. In fact, I am absolutely certain women over forty are the most powerful species on the planet. We are pretty much invincible. And if you are forty-one and reading this and thinking you don't feel like this: fear not. It is coming.

Women sometimes email me (men too, for that matter) to say they wish they had half my confidence, or a little of my courage.

And I reassure them, as I will reassure you: you do have it. You might not feel like it right now, you might feel all at sea and lost in a little boat bobbing about at the behest of every other bastard who needs something from you. But it is coming. The most powerful you, the one like Godzilla with knobs on, is probably just around the corner.

How much of your life do you spend telling other people it will be OK?

When your son falls over and you know his knees are going to be a car crash and will probably make you want to vomit, what's the first thing you say? 'It's going to be OK.'

When your teenager dreads bad test results and is worried

about just how terrible they will actually be, and you know she is off-the-scale autistic and hasn't a cat's chance in hell of emotionally interpreting a passage of English literature, what do you say? 'It will be OK.'

When your husband finds a massive lump the size of a golf ball in his neck, which you immediately assume is cancer that will have spread to his brain, and that you'll see him dead within a year? 'It's going to be OK.'

Strangely enough, even though we see the ultimate doom facing ourselves and those we love time after time, we somehow always manage to tell them that 'it will be OK'. No matter how uncertain the outcome, no matter how terrible the worst-case scenario or how bad it may get, no matter if your house is 'raining on the inside', to quote a neighbour of mine, looking in through my kitchen window when all our water pipes burst… We know it will be OK because one thing we can guarantee is that we will be there to sort it.

Women over forty might know it is going to be grim, but we also know we will make it better somehow. And even if we can't, we will be right there beside our loved ones, and we will laugh at the grimness together.

In intensive care, after my brain surgery, I remember my husband having to hold the drain stitched into my head, and the cardboard toilet under my bits as I crouched on the bed on all-fours to try to have my first wee post-catheter, and then needing him to turn on a tap to try to help me make it come.

In those moments – the furthest from the bride in her dress, or the hot date in matching underwear where you put out like a teenager – in those moments we are defined by the relationships we have invested in and built.

But we never tell ourselves 'it will be OK'. When disaster looms or our lives feel a mess, or we fall in a heap on the floor, or have an interview we are sure we are too rubbish for, we don't give ourselves the same care we offer to everyone else.

We don't look ourselves in the eye or talk to the monster in our head, the paranoid voice that says we are too young, too ugly, too inexperienced, too shy, too not as good as everyone else, and tell it to shut up, tell it everything will be OK, no matter what.

And we should. That same strong woman you are for your family, your husband, your partner, your teenage kids, your baby on the floor with scraped knees – you can be that strong woman for yourself.

I am going to be OK. I can do this. I may as well enjoy this, otherwise what the hell is the point?

Forty is not a moment in time. It is a chapter of life, and your pages will turn and suddenly you will be here too. With us. In the Big-Boobers' club.

I don't mean that in a literal sense, clearly. As we know, mine barely make a B cup unless I lean forward and hoof them up hopefully, in defiance of Newton and all his gravity nonsense.

Being a Big-Boober is a state of mind. A destination we arrive at quite by chance. A way of being that makes us pretty darn invincible.

It requires one key trait, and it's not about being female or somewhere over the arbitrary age of forty. It is simply about not giving a stuff what other people think.

I don't mean all the time, or about everything, and certainly not in a law-breaking, anarchic, sad-bastard, Antifa protestor way.

Obviously you should care what your parents think, whether they are happy or proud, whether your boss thinks you have done a good job, whether your team at work is happy. You want the people around you to be positive about having you in their life.

Not giving a shit about what people think is about limiting what you worry about to things that *actually matter*.

At the age of personal freedom, you stop giving a shit about being judged for the decisions you make, the clothes you wear, and the underwear you put on or not.

You no longer give two hoots about the judgement of those whose sole aim in life is to try to make themselves feel better by making others feel worse. And if occasionally bitter biatches manage to get to you, to break through a chink in your armour or catch you off guard, you can quickly reel yourself back in and shake them off.

You don't care if your handbag has a logo on it or not as long as it has that handy zippy bit where you keep the things that matter. And you can run with it, or it can double as a potty if you are caught short.

You have learned that it really doesn't matter whether you were invited to the hen do or the wedding. In fact, by now, you'd really rather you weren't. Unless you really love them, spending your own cash to watch someone feel pleased with themselves in an over-priced dress with an ugly bridesmaid is not actually a choice you want to make.

Ditto re spending two days in a bloody dressing gown pretending to relax in some infernal, chlorine-belching 'spa' during a drizzly weekend in Cornwall, drinking water with one manky strawberry in it.

We were over this a long time ago.

We were over worrying about baking a cake for the school bake sale or providing party bags for multiple spoiled brats who were never grateful for them anyway.

We were over trying to keep our eyebrows a certain shape or colour. As long as they don't completely meet in the middle, we have done well.

Frankly, we are now focused on our 'tache or our beard – facial hair, like everything, goes south. And none of us wants to be the old lady with the weird black hair on her chin no one told her about.

(I remember a girl at school whose mum had a fairly respectable beard growing on her chin. She wore a headscarf to try to hide it under the knot, but it really only made the problem worse. I wonder how that girl got on in life. Heidi, she was called. I worry her mother's beard may have scarred her for life.)

We don't give a shit if our right tit is bigger than our left, if we have a squaddie shower involving no water and masses of deodorant, or if we piss ourselves every time we sneeze.

Frankly, we Big-Boobers were over such things a long time ago.

We sit here with our podgy middle belly, or our extra

flappy bingo wings, or a saggy bit of back fat overhanging our bra strap and we are alright about it. We are proud of our bodies and what they have gone through and recovered from.

Mine has a bit of gauze to keep my hernia in, otherwise my intestines would hang down my left leg. I have scars where moles thought to be cancerous were cut out, a fractured C5 disk in my back from an old injury, I need to have both arm sockets rebuilt from my hips and am missing part of my skull. Not to mention having had a cumulative 26lbs of child weight shoved out my foof without needing a single stitch. My body is not a temple – it's a punch bag. And it is still standing.

The Big-Boobers are all still standing. And we don't really give a shit whether anyone thinks our arse looks big in this or not.

We can accept we have pubes everywhere. One of mine grows out of a mole at the top of my left inner thigh and could easily double as dental floss if anyone happened to be down there with a bit of pork stuck between two molars.

And, if I am being totally candid, I swear like a seaman.

I have been caught drying my armpits with a Dyson hand drier and, before you ask, yes, it was one of the blade ones you are supposed to glide your hands in and out of. Except I was trying to get my torso in and out of it. There is no comeback from a humiliation like that. You just have to own it.

Sweaty pits! Smile and sashay.

Pretending is exhausting and a bit pathetic. And as much as we admire the young things for keeping up with it all and looking fabulous and hair-free, with their taut little labia and not a pube in sight, we are happier over here. With the other Big-Boobers.

Being young and fabulous is bloody exhausting and expensive. Just to stay on top of looking blisteringly hot and hairless is setting young people back about £150 a month. Price in the hours at minimum wage (which most of them aren't on) and you're topping £300 a month. Just to look prepubescent with hot tits and a perfect brow.

I mean, sod that crap. I'd honestly rather mow my lawn, which is a bit like hoovering but involves a petrol engine and fresh air. I even start mine near the gate of my garden so passers-by can see me revving up my machine; it makes my boobs feel even bigger.

Sometimes I outsource this job to my husband or son – just to show I am the boss, and they are doing this chore at my behest, not because I am a woman and need help with a physical task.

We are over keeping up with things, too. The only thing we really hope to keep up with is the TV drama shown over three weeks on Saturday nights. Or perhaps the supply of toilet paper in the house. We might want to try keeping up with being able to see our girlfriends, or the ironing basket, by ourselves or with help.

But we are, frankly, buggered if you think we are going to try to keep up with the latest jeans or the newest colour for our wardrobes.

You may be doing 'nautical' this summer and schlepping your perfectly pert bottom to Topshop to get something with a chuffing anchor on it. But I can tell you, us Big-Boobers will have something in our wardrobe from four years ago which will now be more on trend than you'll ever be. Whether it fits or not is quite another matter.

Some might imagine that it matters whether they are in boyfriend, girlfriend, skinny or high-waisted jeans. I can tell them, with some authority, none of those labels mean a thing.

It doesn't matter if you want to call your jeans after your boyfriend, your dad or your grandma. (In fact, a grandma jean would be hilarious. Smelling a bit of roast dinners, talcum powder and cabbage, with a side order of wee.) What you need is your favourite jean. The one that looks pretty good, is comfy as hell, and tells you if you are a couple of pounds on the heavier side and need to consider whether profiteroles really are the way forward for the next two weeks.

My favourite jeans just went through at the crotch, which is a royal pain in the arse and now means I need a new pair of favourite jeans – and that doesn't just happen. Jeans evolve. They cannot be bought.

I suspect it has worn through due to the sheer pressure exerted by the heft of my labia, but we can never be sure.

I just read a horrifying article on Mail Online which informed me that girls as young as eleven are seeking surgery for their lady bits to make them look more like they want them to. I say to these girls: stop watching porn and get out more. At eleven, you should be concerned with how fast you can run and which boys you can beat, not whether your dangly bits are too dangly for a boy to insert his pathetic manhood into.

That is a privilege (theirs) and you are the gatekeeper. If

your bits are a bit dangly and make that journey a little trickier, so much the better.

Women over forty don't need to follow trends or worry so much about being 'perfect'. We don't want to be the best; we only want to be the best version of ourselves. Or at least a vaguely acceptable one.

If we do end up covered in vomit, or have slightly wet ourselves laughing, we want a forgiving friend.

Many things make the Big-Boobers fearless. Sex, for starters.

When you are younger, sex is bloody exhaustion. Sheer effort and hard work. The endless pursuit of it, foxy withholding of it, tempting with it, and trying to only give it to the right people.

Then there's the performance itself.

I have done things in my past I would never do now. Unless I was unconscious and they were done without my knowledge, in which case some git would have questions to answer when I came to.

These days unconscious sex is very frowned upon, and for good reason. Consent is, indeed, everything. Although I would suggest if you are getting a form to seek written consent, as at some American university campuses, things may have gone a little too far in the other direction.

I am absolutely in favour of sexual safety. But I can see there being some turn-off in reaching for a clipboard and a biro to get your prize pull to sign up for a session with your good self.

I can reflect fondly on my time in bed doing things other

than sleeping. And I can laugh at myself, and at the nonsense of it all, without regretting a thing.

I've jiggled about athletically on top, while trying to stick my tiny nipples into his mouth. I've sucked on bits without gagging while trying to dangle my bits into his mouth without suffocating him. I've stood on tippy toes trying to pretend to be utterly uninhibited, with a cooker hood banging against my head and the gas bottle rammed in my front bottom. And I've pretended to enjoy sex on a flight of stairs during an act so physically forceful one of the banisters snapped in two. (I put it back together and pretended it was all fine. I apologise to the subsequent homeowner for this flagrant breach of health and safety, which I have never reported.)

Now I would quite happily turn my back, pull down my jimjams and let Mark crack on while I catch a few extra winks or get my makeup off with a Superdrug face wipe.

If he is enjoying himself and I am able to multi-task, we're having a good time together, even if we're doing slightly different things.

Like a holiday, where I can go to the gym and he can play tennis: both active, but in different ways.

It's not that I care less. It's that I care more about the things that matter. And the things actually within my control.

I don't want anyone to like me more by pretending to be something I am not. Pretending to be a porn star in pretty pants and matching bra just isn't up there on my list of priorities – or, indeed, even on the list.

My most erotic fantasy right now probably involves a roast dinner and a bottle of wine, a really hard mattress with my own pillow, and a cuddle with my husband while we watch a funny film in bed together.

I appreciate your own sex life may be far more adventurous than mine. And I do not pretend to speak for the love lives of all Big-Boobers. Some women I know are still dangling off bedposts doing it every other night. One girlfriend still allows her husband anal on birthdays and Christmas. As soon as the advent calendars come out, I think of her and wince. Santa very much comes up the chimney to give her a present in her house. Either she is a brave woman and is taking one for the team, or she's showing the rest of us up for being the selfish cows we really are. Perhaps I just don't value my marriage *that* much. Or maybe, if her husband needs to put it somewhere he shouldn't, he should stick it in an apple pie in the bakery aisle at Tesco.

Whatever we women are doing between the sheets, we own it, and own the phases of it. It may we'll be that by the time you are reading this I will be going through a dominatrix phase. By day, a lesbian bookseller from Brighton. By night, a fierce bedroom warrior, nipples pinched tight by clamps, an orange in my gob, more buckles than a boot store, locked into a metal girdle with only my front bottom on show.

I don't see that in my future right now. But I am not saying it can't happen. I don't feel frightened of what might happen in my future, either.

In a mad world, where I don't really know what I am doing from one week to the next and I remain acutely aware of how the hands of fate can play cruel tricks on all of us, I feel re-markably in control.

The things that matter most of all in life to me are solid. And if they get a bit broken, I will tell them it will be OK and I will fix them. Or be right there through the grim bits, holding their hands.

If my jobs change, or I get fired, or my boss leaves and I need to leave too, that will be alright as well. This has been an adventure, there will be a new one around the corner. And you never know, it may be even more powerful. Just look at Sarah and Lucy, owning their choices and their lives at work.

When I feel frightened, or question whether I can do something, or whether I am strong enough, I can now look in the mirror and tell myself it will be OK. I have seen worse, done worse, survived worse. I'm still standing.

And bugger me, if I am going to do something, I may as well enjoy it and go for broke. If it all goes wrong, I will fix it. And if someone doesn't like it, it gives me great pleasure to inform them that I couldn't give a shit what they think.

WHAT MAKES US HUMAN

Three score years and ten, my dad says. Then you'll have done well.

I remind him he'll be seventy in November and we talk about the weather instead.

That's a British thing, isn't it? Not to talk about it – not to talk about death. Trying to make sense of it with numbers, rational stuff we can understand.

Others embrace death as the natural order of things, a simple change of form. From present to eternal, physical to ethereal.

But not us; ours is the errant uncle. The one who ended up in the papers. The one we don't talk about any more.

I've never known it. Never had a death in the family I was old enough to understand. Nor lost a friend to cancer. Never spent a silent vigil watching someone breathe. Holding my own breath when theirs stops for a moment too long.

I've been to funerals. Watched others try to do a reading, and return to their seat, throat burning, silenced by sadness.

Seen people tiptoe around it, buy sympathy cards, sit, pen in hand, in their kitchen, made illiterate by the awkwardness of it all, finding big words too hard to write.

My girlfriends talk about their mums, now gone. About leaving them, absolutely, for the first time in their lives. Girlfriends with mums just like my own, who I call every night at seven just to offload the day.

Nothing chats, useless chats, boring chats – but perfect all the same. A moan about your dad, or the parcel delivery you waited in all day for. The tomatoes that refuse to ripen.

The tiny stuff of life.

You say you'd give anything to have that one last phone call with your mum. Just one more chance to chat about nothing in particular but everything that matters just the same.

You say that if she hadn't left so suddenly you'd have ended your final conversation with 'love you', just to say it one last time.

Some save old messages on their phone, to listen to when they feel most alone.

Others stand crying in the kitchen, reaching out for familiar fingers, soft and worn by the garden, wishing her to reach back and say everything will be OK, or to serve up a roast dinner that will make the world seem right again.

Or ring her old number, just to hear it ring. Just to believe for a second she might pick up, imagining her, grumbling from the kitchen over her tea going cold.

Lovely. Grumpy. Funny. Mum.

The thing we all share in this journey between life and death is that we are not ready. We're too young to take on the mantle of the elders. Not wise enough to know why this cake didn't rise, or that the baby's rash will be OK. Why these roast potatoes look so awful or whether the kids will ever put the top back on the toothpaste or squeeze it from the bottom.

I reach down for my tiny son's hand as we cross the road, hoping always that a little paw will still reach up for mine, still need me as we face the flow.

And I reach up for my mum's, holding on tight as the sands of time run faster and faster. Making sure I tell her I love her at seven each night.

And others of you reach even further. Standing on tiptoe now, straining to reach your mum, your nan, no longer here but still sitting happily in your memories and the pictures on your kitchen wall. That funny day when you all got soaked by rain on a walk. Or when she snored through the Queen's Speech she was so adamant she wanted to watch.

That's the funny thing. Whether we are together or apart, alive or not, here in this place or another, we still walk together. Separated, but all joined up. One behind the other, yet part of this big circle we call life.

My father says one dies to make way for another. All matter of fact. But then he tells me the doctors can take anything but not his eyes. The big softie.

He'll be watching, you see.

I like to believe we move to a place just next door, watching, waiting, smiling. At the end of the phone we cannot answer.

I tell my children I will always be here for them. No matter what. Mummy will always be there watching.

You know, death does not define us. Nor the awkward silence we baptise it in.

It is our longing to hear that trusted voice at the end of the line, to chat to the one we still love about the small stuff that matters not, to tell mum that we love her one last time.

It is the way we walk forward hand in hand with the ones who left us behind that defines us and makes us most human.

CHAPTER 10

YOUR BIG FAT FRIEND

I don't hate fat people.

I honestly don't. I don't wish them ill, I don't point and laugh, and I don't think they are any less than me because they are twice the size – of me, or maybe even of a bus.

In fact, as with so much in life, I just want to change them and make them better.

What I am, however, is a bit fat-fixated. If there is a fat person in my vicinity, I see them. If they are very fat, I watch them. And I do tend to stare.

I am not obsessed with fat people. But I am fixated by them.

I simply cannot believe we live in a time when there is so little scarcity, so little shame and such little need for physical endeavour that we are now twice, three times or more the size we should be.

It baffles me every day that we have so much machinery, so much sedentary work, so little to physically sweat about, and yet we have carried on eating as if we were all potato farmers in the bleak highlands, having to break the frozen soil with an axe to plant a bloody spud, desperate for calories wherever they can be found.

And I find it bonkers – as in standing-up, stamping-my-feet, swearing-as-I-walk-across-the-room bonkers – that when we find ourselves so fat it takes two seats to accommodate our vast arses, we don't do anything about it. We just keep on eating and expect the world to accommodate our new size.

And it does. The world has changed. The world is normalising fat. Fat is the new normal.

We have extra-wide shoes on sale everywhere as feet become flattened by the enormous load they are obliged to carry.

I can't get a 6.5 shoe, which is my *actual* size. As in, the actual size of my real foot. But if I were a massive chubster and my feet were size 6.5 wide, there would be no problem.

There are fat clothes, the result of sizing shifting ever upwards. An old 8 is now called a 16. Skinny jeans are available in a size 24.

Just for the record, chubsters, those are not *skinny* jeans. They just feature the word 'skinny'. To be fair, a pair of boyfriend extra baggies would have the same effect on your oil-rig legs – they just wouldn't sound as nice when you bought them.

Like benevolent parents, the high street accommodates our fat feet, our fat bodies, even our fat faces. I asked Specsavers whether they have had to make plus-size frames as our faces have got fatter; a new 'comfort fit' is indeed available.

And the high street has seen fit to also accommodate our fat kids.

It is one of the biggest tragedies of our time that instead of facing this chronic obesity plague head on, we are normalising it in the most British of fashions, as politely and as quietly as possible.

Plus-size kids' school uniforms hit Marks and Spencer nearly a decade ago. Obviously we can't call them plus-size as we might be in danger of hurting the feelings of the precious mini walruses. Instead, the uniforms are called 'sturdy' or 'growing kids', making it sound like they are for strong and robust children, as opposed to weaklings covered in blubber.

If you listen to my language, you'll understand where the line became blurred between feeling nothing but hurt for fat people, and hating fat people.

I am blunt and direct (which can be seen as hurtful in itself). We are not used to hearing fat people called chubsters, though it is my friendly term.

Frankly, as much as I might be slightly obsessed with your size, it is your life, and if you want to balls it up by eating KFC every Friday and failing to go for a walk afterwards, I can accept my opinion is worth nothing to you. It is easier to assume I hate fat people so that I am the one with the problem and in the wrong.

But I don't and I am not. There is no right or wrong in this. There is only a problem, and a problem we can't start to solve unless we talk about it.

When children are involved, then I am properly angry. Not just a bit cross but properly, full-on raging. And given that love and hate are two things that live side by side, my tears of anger fall thick and fast over fat kids.

In America, shooting my film *My Fat Story*, I was doing a section in a burger joint and watched massive parents feeding massive burgers into their morbidly obese children on a Saturday lunchtime.

I lost the plot. I went outside and was a tear-strewn mess in seconds.

My director, who was filming, kept asking what the hell I was doing – 'Is this for real? Are you alright?' – while I had a full-scale meltdown over the two enormous kids being force-fed burgers.

He had never seen me cry before. Assumed I was the super-tough woman people imagine me to be. Forgot I am a mum, forgot I don't hate fat people, that I just can't understand them. He missed the real me entirely.

Fat children make me weep. They make me cry tears of sadness and anger all at once. I want to go up to the parents at the seaside as they lie like beached whales behind their chubby children, uncomfortable in their overstretched swim-suits, and ask what the bloody hell they think they are doing.

And what goddamn right they think they have to do this to their children.

How has it become acceptable in 21st-century Britain to feed your kids to death? Or fail to help them exercise enough that they stay fit enough to do more?

It is the same at the school gate. I cannot bear the sight of fat kids stumbling out of the car, dropped off by parents who don't even get out, and typically have one arm hanging from the window, weighed down by little fat parcels of their own.

They don't just park near the school gate, of course. They park on top of it to minimise the amount of exercise their child might be in danger of taking that day.

My personal bias might encourage me to think this is a state-school-only problem, reserved for the lazy sods who think everything is free so you might as well abuse it.

But I would be wrong. Parents at my kids' private school also drive right up to the school building, if not on top of it, idling on the double yellows so their precious little flowers won't have to walk the terrifying 100 metres to a spot where everyone is at significantly reduced odds of getting run over or squashed.

We have grown ridiculous in our ability to be lazy.

Parents allowing their children to become obese before they can even begin to make their own choices is nothing short of child cruelty.

If a child turns up for school underweight, unfed and looking uncared for, social services are involved. I know of teachers who bring food into class to make sure these children have something to eat that day.

If we saw a horribly emaciated child at the beach, our moral decency would prompt us to act (although these poor wretches are more often locked in rooms and hidden away).

Yet it's socially acceptable to parade about kids at the opposite end of the weight spectrum, who are arguably just as abused.

We have kids rocking up to primary school already obese at the age of four or five – and nothing is said. One child in ten starts school overweight or obese.

I think I need to shout this louder to make people hear: one child in ten turns up at school – three in an average class – barely out of their buggy and yet already overweight or obese.

You have to wonder how they are not getting enough exercise to burn that stuff off.

Young kids of four and five are maniacs. My personal parenting style for kids of that age is to think of them like dogs:

they need to be fed, watered, and allowed to run free twice a day every day. It seems that many children aren't that lucky.

I wonder as well what precisely the tech industry thinks it is playing at, encouraging kids to use gadgets at four and five. I don't want to hear your lame-arsed excuses that the toys are educational or 'great for long plane journeys'. So are books, but I don't see your kid with one of those.

You can't be arsed. And the electronic LeapPad you bought for your four-year-old shuts your kid up.

That's the truth of it. And it is your decision. Marketeers might have made you feel better about it, and given you the nudge to buy it and the permission to feel OK about it, but you own the decision. They are merely pandering to your guilt because you know what I have said is the truth and you need an excuse.

There is no excuse. Your kid needs to be run like a dog – preferably on a beach or field or somewhere wild. Definitely not a shopping centre.

Everything else is just a sticking plaster.

You also have to question what the hell parents are feeding their children to make them obese aged twelve … or even four. How is it possible that before a child is able to make any real decisions about the way they live their lives, they are already shovelling down more calories than they can burn in a day, and failing to develop any of the muscles that would help them burn the weight off?

So I asked. I asked the nurses and the community midwives. And the answers are too weird to believe.

Mothers purée their own food for the baby.

Standard – so did most of us. If I made a roast, I made extra veg so I could whizz up a few dinners for the girls.

But these mothers are puréeing the food *they* eat. So if it's KFC or Chinese takeaway, the baby is getting KFC and Chinese takeaway too. Same with curry, or burger and chips. It all becomes baby's food as well. Via a blender and a spoon.

You may say this can't be true. But it's not coming from me. It's coming from the healthcare professionals.

And if you want evidence of it in action, look at the state of the babies once these mothers have fed them for four years of their lives.

Of course this is personal. It is deeply personal. Children are personal.

Criticise my children and I can already feel my neck muscles tighten, my back straighten and myself grow a foot as I prepare to wade in and defend them. That's pure parental instinct kicking in.

(Although I will add the caveat that my overriding instinct is to blame my kids first and then work backwards from there. This has served me well to date.)

But if you criticise my child for being fat, you are not only criticising my baby; you are criticising me. A double personal attack at the thing I feel acutely passionate about.

So it follows that no one dares say anything. No one dares to challenge these parents about the state of their kids. Or ask the kids how it has come about that they are carrying around two of themselves on a pair of knees built for one.

Doctors don't address it in their surgeries because they only have a seven-minute window per appointment and no one wants to take on another problem. Teachers don't address it because it is a sensitive issue – and many of them are overweight themselves. Family and friends don't address it because they are part of the problem, too.

Everything is set up to ignore the literal elephant in the room.

We tiptoe around the problem, resize everything to make people feel better, and enforce school learning about how we are all different, diversity is a positive thing, and bullying is the devil.

It is a great thing that we are all different. But not when that difference is an extra twenty inches around the waist and an extra three stone to heft about on the way to geography class. That is not diversity. That is obesity-acceptance. And I think it is plain wrong.

The popular consensus enforced by everyone from the body-beautiful brigade to plus-size to feminism to government legislation is that it is fattist to say anything.

Fattist is a made-up word, of course, to join the long list of other 'ist' words used to label people with whom you disagree.

There were discussions about making it illegal to be fattist, that it was a hate crime just like any other. And there have been successful legal cases brought by individuals who believe their employer has discriminated against them on the basis of their weight.

I don't consider it to be discriminatory not to employ someone because of their weight. It reflects a simple commercial reality. Or, in my case, a personal choice.

I would not want to share a space with someone massively overweight because everything they did would set me off. If they moved too slowly, huffed when they sat down, moaned when they got up, ate all the time or noisily, or smelled in the heat, I would rue the day I ever thought they might be good at their job.

I also don't think a fat person could do my job as well as I could. They couldn't whip across town, jump on a train, leg it out the Underground, change outfits quickly, and pretend to be calm under bright light; their sheer size would make these things virtually impossible to perform and certainly impossible to sustain.

This is not discrimination. It is a consequence of their own actions.

When I went on the *This Morning* sofa and told a large lady to her face that I would not employ her because she was too fat – said without malice, honestly, looking straight at her – people were outraged.

The lady and I got on well, before and after our appearance together. In many ways she respected the fact that I helped her to air her side of the argument too, and she didn't say one thing off-camera and another thing on it.

We both had our say. Thousands agreed with me. Millions didn't. And it became the start of my public journey with fat people. Them assuming I hated them. Me saying what I thought without tiptoeing around the truth.

Others have made efforts to address the issue.

There was and is a government programme to measure the height and weight of children in school and identify the scale of the problem. Overweight children are identified and parents are given the results.

However, parents responded angrily to being told their child was overweight, often rejecting it outright.

Instead of working out how to tackle the gulf between reality and parental views, the official instruction was to change the communications. Children were no longer classified as 'obese', but 'very overweight'.

By the time you read this it would not surprise me if even trying to tell parents their kids are too fat has been stopped on the grounds that it offends sensitivities and is fattist.

As many as one third of mums and dads don't know their own child is overweight. They do not recognise their child is fat.

We use friendly terms like puppy fat, baby weight, love handles – language aimed at making being fat a cuddly, friendly thing. Instead of saying, 'I am/you are a fat, lazy bastard.'

So children with puppy fat grow into being big boys or big girls and the urban myth that it is 'in my genes' and all the Joneses are 'big-boned' lives on.

These are just excuses in a long list of excuses. And believe me, I have heard them all. The list of reasons why you are not to blame for being fat is truly epic, and represents one of the greatest cop-outs of our time.

With their excuses for why being the size they are is definitely not their fault, chubsters have cornered the market in a culture where personal responsibility has lost all meaning and the way to get ahead is to invent a bigger cover-up or better excuse than the next person.

I am not to blame because:

There is a lack of education about the right stuff to eat. I mean, this whole five-a-day healthy-eating thing is still a relatively new concept and, like cigarettes, none of us knew that eating KFC and Chinese takeaway every other night in front of the telly could be bad for us. Literally, no one ever mentioned it.

Bull. You know and I know that if you love it, it is probably bad for you. And if you love it that much, it's probably only something you should eat once a week max, and earn with exercise.

Healthy food is really expensive. Look at the price of fruit. It is much cheaper to feed my kids these eighteen pizzas and frozen waffles than puréed kiwi fruit smoothie. I cannot afford to feed my family healthily. I can only afford frozen chips and chicken nuggets.

Bull. The only thing missing in this equation is effort. I won't buy my family raspberries or strawberries because they are overpriced. But fruit being expensive is a different fact from you being too idle to cook a meal from scratch. The real reason you buy packaged crap is not because it is cheap, it's because it involves zero effort and you can't be arsed. You are not fat because pizza is cheap. You are fat because you couldn't be bothered to make a chilli.

There is too much hidden sugar in everything. One can of coke has eight teaspoons of sugar. We can't help being fat if we are force-fed sugar.

Bull. You know all this and are still drinking it. You are making bad choices. You need to own your decisions. Drinking full-sugar coke is a shortcut to being a fat person.

*Schools have sold all their playing fields and there is no exercise
taught in school any more so my kid never gets a run.*
True. But bull all the same.

It is a monumental disaster that some schools decided to sell
their playing fields and, born out of a drive to abolish any form of
competition for fear of causing offence to a precious little flower,
the idea of sport has all but disappeared in state primaries.

It turns out kids quickly lose interest in sport when they
are not challenged or can never win. Or when every sport is
a team challenge, and the teams include the whippets who
never get to run free. My own kids had ten minutes of 'shake
and shine' at the start of a school day, performed in their
school uniform and led by the same class teacher they would
be with all day, who didn't want to be there.

It is true that most state schools are hopeless at delivering
sport. I would argue many primaries now avoid it altogether.

But it is bull to use this as an excuse. Knowing school is
failing your child is not a good enough reason for you to fail
your child too. If school doesn't provide exercise, the onus is
on you to provide it. You can't simply throw up your hands
and give up.

*It's a family thing. She's got the Johnson arse. He's got the Will-
mot thighs. We are all big boned.*
Bull. No one has big bones. And your family surname is not
code for a whole new type of arse or thighs.

No matter what shape you are genetically predisposed to
be – even if your mother is a short-arse and you are therefore
only five foot two – you still control the food that goes into

your face and the distance you run. Or, more significantly, your children's faces and whether or not they run at all.

Fat families are all fat together because they eat the same crap, have the same exercise routine (none), don't guilt each other into doing something about it, and accept that because mum is fat they will be fat too.

Some research suggests there is a gene which predisposes you to gain weight. But it can only get going on turning you into a chubster if you let it. My kid might be predisposed to piss himself in public spaces at the age of three. My job is to show him this is not on.

I maintain that in the shadow of every fat kid is a fat parent. Excuses won't cut it with me.

It's time. There is no time to exercise. My day is so busy, I don't stop from the minute I get up to the minute I go to bed. There is no way I would find time for a run or a class.
Bull. There is time. But you will have to make it. And you will have to change a couple of things to make it happen. Show me your day, I will show you the time. Sleep next to your sports kit, walk two stops before you get the bus, march in the ad breaks, get up fifteen minutes earlier, do the school run on foot, park three streets away and walk the last bit.

The gym is too expensive.
Bull. Go and look out a window. There is your gym. Actual gyms are too expensive; they are also too poncy, too filled with plonkers and mirrors, and too conducive to chatting rather than doing. They also encourage people to buy fashionable

items to go to the gym in. Which has about as much to do with exercise as eating KFC. Buying a new pair of Sweaty Betty leggings does not make you fitter, even if you reckon it makes your arse look hot.

My medication messes with my weight.
Not good enough – although, believe me, I empathise. For twenty years of my life I have taken industrial quantities of epilepsy medication: 2,000 mg of Keppra, 1,500 mg of Tegretol (that's the maximum dose). Plus an upper to counter the downer of Keppra. Plus contraceptive jabs in my arse.

Meds are not a competition. And I am certainly not trying to get one up on anyone with a health condition. But meds are not an excuse. They are a fact of our lives. A fact we need to take into account when we are standing facing the fridge. You are still in control, and you still have choices.

Even if your epilepsy has just dislocated both your shoulders and your Keppra makes you want to kill yourself. You have to control the bits you can, even if those bits feel really tiny.

I have a hyperactive/hypoactive thyroid.
Understood. Do you also have a pair of trainers?

I am part of the body-positive movement. I am beautiful inside and out. And plus-size just means there is more of me to love. What? This stick? This is because my knees are buggered.
Bull. You are trying to be positive about the body you have eaten yourself into. And undoubtedly you are a beautiful person. But

we can also be honest: your buggered knees are not a coincidence and the stick you are walking with is a physical clue about what you are doing to yourself. I was invited to the plus-size awards for 'disservices to fat people' and went to collect my trophy just to piss them off. The thing that burned itself onto my retinas – apart from the fourteen-stone ladies in bikinis for the swimwear round – was the number of sticks in the room. They were leaning on chairs, against tables – I couldn't move for sticks. Even the judges had them. Fat women applauding other fat women while their sticks leaned within easy reaching distance to support the room full of crippled knees and hips.

To be clear, I am not mocking, sneering, pointing or laughing. I went to the plus-size awards because I was invited. And I am not a coward. Being morbidly obese is a hard place to be. But I am calling bull on the argument that you should be positive about it, and should whoop and applaud each other in your swimming costumes. You should not be ashamed; shame helps no one. You should be honest.

I am fat and happy.
I understand why we are quick to buy into this explanation. It is a way of avoiding the issue all together. Accept you are fat. Laugh your way around it and get on with more important stuff in life.

Except you are not fat and happy when you are trying to get dressed for a night out with your girlfriends. You are not fat and happy when you want to try on clothes. You are not fat and happy when you get naked or want to go swimming or have to run up the stairs. You are a happy person *apart* from the times you are crucified by feeling frumpy and horrible.

And that's OK, too. But being honest and admitting that you would be happier if you were less fat is the starting point for everything.

Only when we reach the point of being able to admit that there are no excuses can we start to find a solution. The day you are able to look in a mirror and say, 'I am fat, I have a problem, I own this problem' – that's the day you can begin to address it.

There is a whole army of people out there willing to help you. You don't need more money, or more time, or childcare, or to stop taking your meds. You only need to change two things: move a lot more, eat a bit less.

I know it sounds easy for someone like me, someone who is lucky to be skinny, someone who likes running, who has a functional relationship with food. There are emotional reasons for the ways we eat and the shapes we are. But having embraced all of that, and all the excuses I've heard for why it is easy for me but not for you, I know it can be done.

I was so certain of it and felt so strongly about it that I set out to prove it. I decided to put my money where my mouth is. I went to a production company and told them I had an idea.

I would put on four stone and lose it again, to prove fat people are lazy and I am not lucky to be thin. Simples.

For the next six months of my life I filmed *My Fat Story*. It turned out to be one of the hardest things I have ever done.

CHAPTER 11

FAT STORY

' I will put on four stone and lose it again to prove fat people are lazy.'

I wondered why my agent was looking at me like she was going to kill me when we got outside. It wouldn't have been the first time, but she did look especially cross.

Commissioned by the big bosses in TV land within ten days, *My Fat Story* became a thing before I knew it.

In TV world, nothing happens this fast. No idea ever gets off the table this quickly. A thousand good ideas are rejected before one makes it through for further discussion. And even the one that sneaks through to the next level usually gets crushed to death a few months down the line at the whim of some commissioning editor.

The speed of this decision-making was not the only frightening thing; the reality of what was involved also started to kick in and scare the hell out of me, too.

It was all very well sitting in a meeting room with TV people chatting about my frustrations at the endless list of excuses used by fat people. When an actual contract arrived, binding me to make the programme and gain four stone in weight, I did wonder, as so many other times in my life, just what the hell I was doing.

My mother, an ever-unreliable source of wisdom, thought it was a terrible idea. She has always banged on about me being too skinny, but even she thought putting on weight for a programme was lunacy. And this is the same woman who thought *Celebrity Big Brother* was a good idea.

I told my mates. The usual reaction from women was how blooming nice it would be to eat whatever the hell I wanted whenever the hell I felt like it, and to eat as much of it as possible with no limits.

Which I found odd, because I pretty much did that anyway. I have never been on a diet and have never tried to lose weight.

At the time I signed to *My Fat Story*, I ate about six small meals a day, a couple of chocolate bars on the run, about six sugared coffees, and any other snacks I felt like in between.

I ran once a day and generally legged it about on a bike or on foot to meetings or school runs or down to the train station to get up to London.

That's how I see myself when I look back: this running-around thing continually stuffing things in her face to keep going.

I am useless when I am hungry, grumpy when I have to wait for food. I turn into a wobbly wreck if I can't get sugar when I need it. After a run, I will eat a bun from the cake shop over the road and drink a sugary coffee. I often munch on a Dairy Milk when I work.

As I was to learn, I have a functional relationship with food, much like a car and petrol. I don't eat because I really love food; I eat because it keeps me running and I conk out really quickly without it.

That's the reason no one really knows I was on *I'm a Celebrity... Get Me Out of Here!* in the jungle with Ant and Dec. For one thing, I was not really a celebrity, just a poxy ex-*Apprentice* who had no right to be there. And for another, I was rubbish. As in perfectly rubbish. The challenges didn't scare me. I was in a glass coffin filled with cockroaches, lowered over a gorge, and I wasn't that bothered. But more than that, I was dull as hell. Properly dull. Without food, I am essentially even duller than Clare Balding. Or an ugly Tess Daly with even less personality.

Other people, like Christopher Biggins, with whom I shared my jungle time, were brilliant without food. In fact, he positively thrived on it. He went into the jungle with diabetes, high blood pressure, heart issues and all manner of other complaints. He even had a special chair to sit on and I was his chair helper-inner and helper-outer because he couldn't easily do either on his own.

Three weeks later, having shifted God knows how many stone through starvation, he was still hilarious, having a wonderful time, and able to hop in and out of that chair of his own accord. The jungle was great for him. But terrible for me.

I do see that others have a very different relationship with food. And I do get it. Not physically, but I do watch in wonderment. Maybe you are the same. Maybe you get a menu in a restaurant and imagine eating all of it. And could eat all of it. Maybe you spend ages reading the menu, imagining how each dish will taste or remembering where you've had something like that before.

My foodie friends do this. They can hardly bring them-selves to choose because everything sounds delicious to them and by choosing one thing they might miss out on another. They might even ask what something comes with, or whether it has this or that on it, to help them decide.

I find myself watching them like a cat with its head on one side. Wondering what these strange human types are doing with their funny book of food and their dribbling mouths.

People offer all sorts of excuses for why *My Fat Story* was easy for me (and would therefore be impossible for them), but the only one I understand and agree with to some extent is that my relationship with food is purely practical.

My response, however, to every excuse is: imagine the size of the challenge for someone like me. First, for someone not that interested in food to have to eat enough of it to gain half of my normal body weight; second, to quickly pile that weight onto a frame not used to being fat.

Not to mention the size of the challenge for someone with an intense relationship to exercise. And now I was to have none. I didn't appreciate at the start of my story just how in-tense that relationship was. It can be compared to a chubster's relationship with food: hugely emotional.

And so my journey began. The simple premise was to gain four stone – three months to put it on, three months to get it off.

As part of this journey I was to meet people who struggle with their weight, to challenge chubsters with my views, and to see what happened to my belief that fat people are lazy.

But my fundamental reason for *My Fat Story* was to prove

that there are no excuses. If you want to be less fat, you have to eat a bit less and move a bit more.

You may not turn into Gisele. You may not be a size zero with a lollipop head and an arse tighter than Victoria Beckham's (who'd want that?). But everyone has it within them to exercise control over their weight, at no cost, if they make the effort.

I set out to prove you are fat because you are lazy, and the day you accept you have a problem and are prepared to own the problem is the day you can fix it. For free.

As I stood in my kitchen having my 'before' shots taken, I did get to wondering what the hell I was doing.

I was wildly epileptic at the time, fitting four or five times a night, occasionally dislocating my arms in the process, and trying to run my own business, write for a national newspaper and be a mum of three children under ten.

There are moments in my life when I think I am actually just a stupid cow with a big gob. And inclined to agree with the 50 per cent of the country who think precisely this.

The photos of me in my revolting pants and bra (chosen deliberately so I didn't look like I loved myself) show me exactly as I see myself: a skinny house brick on two cocktail sticks. I literally need to write 'front' and 'back' on my T-shirt for people to tell one side of me from the other. I have no boobs and no arse.

(Although, as we have discussed, I have very long labial folds, which I never knew before.)

I was already starting to get scared. A few things had dawned on me.

I'd never really had to think about my wardrobe. I'd had the same clothes for years, knew exactly the sorts of dresses that worked on my silly body, and could buy a new one in about two seconds, knowing it would fit.

Size 8 Reiss. Size 10 Karen Millen. Size 8 Whistles. Job done.

I spent three or four nights on the road each week and could pack a suitcase to handle five different functions in about five minutes. Dress x 5. Shoes x 2. Underwear. Tights. Bathroom crap. Makeup. Done.

Putting on weight was about to stuff all that.

Very quickly, things stopped fitting. Everything stopped fitting – apart from me. As an epileptic, the cruel irony was that I was the only thing that fitted any more.

The things I took for granted in life were about to get very difficult indeed. I was about to learn what it is like when weight gets in the way of your world.

Things get harder fast.

I was now eating 6,000 calories a day. At least, I was supposed to be eating 6,000 calories a day. That's the equivalent of four roast dinners plus snacks and high-fat drinks and shakes.

As I've said, my girlfriends' first reaction to this was: lush. The thought of eating whatever the hell you like sounds appealing to most women, which surprises me even now. It's not just that people think it would be nice to eat whatever they fancy, but also the fact that so many women live their lives restricting themselves in some way. Restricting what they eat, or how often they eat it, or don't. Feeling guilty for eating bad stuff, trying to be good.

Fat fact: most women spend most of their lives trying to be

good with food. It is relentless and effortful, and dictates how good or bad you feel about yourself. Which is horrid.

It seems nearly universal. And it's exhausting. I am not criticising it. I had just never realised that for many people every day is a battle with food: trying to be good, beating themselves up for being bad, trying to resist stuff, giving in and regretting it the next day.

That is a lot of brain space and a lot of pleasure and enjoyment replaced with negativity, sadness and misery. For most people, food and emotion are part of the same language.

Within two weeks, my watch stopped fitting on my wrist.

I couldn't get my head around it at first. I thought the strap was broken, that it must have a kink in it. I have stupid little wrists and scrawny little ankles, like a chicken.

But my watch, made of enamel bits and rigid, would no longer do up on my wrist.

Fat fact: I always put weight on 'here' – point to the relevant bit. For me, 'here' turned out to be my waist.

However, when you put weight on your waist/bum/hips, you also get incrementally fatter everywhere else. My watch was my first real marker, before my clothes. I made myself a mental note: the day I was getting back to my normal weight would be the day my watch was comfy on my wrist again.

My day was now centred around food and eating.

I had a milkshake when I woke up, then a breakfast of two croissants and full-fat, high-sugar cereal with full-fat milk, before a chocolate snack at 10 a.m.

I put away my trainers and my running scruffs and stopped legging it about, to concentrate on eating.

The film crew who were going to document my journey began adding stuff to my life. In my kitchen was a snazzy new pair of scales to track my daily weight.

I had never owned scales before. Never really saw the point of looking at a number, because it didn't matter. Like other skinny bitches, I weighed myself by my favourite jeans; as long as they were snug and comfy, I was fine. Weight was nothing in my life.

Fat fact: scales are an evil instrument of torture. I had watched other women and talked with them about scales before. I knew a bit about how the scales relationship worked. I didn't know how brutal and evil it is.

Fat me had to learn that scales can control your emotional life. If the number on the scales is 'good', let's say an arbitrary ten stone, that's good. If it is ten stones two pounds, that's bad.

If you're fourteen stone and reading this, you are already pissed off, because people who weigh ten stone don't realise how bloody lucky they are. You dream of being ten stone.

I get it. I really do. For all of us there is a number, but for some of us, that number governs our day.

I know legions of women who get up in the morning, have a wee, then weigh. And that's the only time they are prepared to set foot on the scales.

Others get up, wee, strip and then weigh.

To them, the idea of stepping on scales fully dressed is ridiculous; they look at you like you have just asked them to have sex with a sheep. Like you are a proper pervert. Weigh with clothes on? Who are you, Jimmy frigging Savile?

Some move their feet out of bed straight onto the scales, as they are lighter that way. I have even heard from women who shave and dry their hair before weighing because they're sure that takes off a pound or two.

Most women I know won't weigh after 9 a.m., not ever.

And some will avoid weighing themselves if they had a meal out where they ate pudding and know it will be bad news. Bad news means one pound over their accepted weight.

Others tell me their day is ruined first thing if they step on the scales and it is bad; they spend the day feeling fat and depressed, particularly if they had made an effort to be 'good' the day before.

After all, if you are going to be 'good' and end up putting on three pounds, what is the bloody point? You may as well be 'bad' and save yourself the effort.

I see this now. I have had a glimpse into a whole world I never knew existed. And I hate that women feel this way.

Fat fact: scales are exhausting and our relationship with them is cruel.

By now I was eating constantly. Six thousand calories requires a dedicated approach to eating. Particularly if you are someone who doesn't think about food unless they are hungry. I had a food schedule and a food diary.

I was measuring my weight and taking a daily selfie in my underwear, and my husband was stalking me with a camera to get clips of me talking about my progress.

I was not doing well.

Stopping running was killing me. I hadn't really understood the relationship I had with the road. My forty-minute run was never about losing weight or staying fit. It turns out it kept me sane and made me a relatively bearable person to live with. I was tolerable after a run.

I knew I ran when I was pissed off. And I knew I ran when I was angry. I also knew I could run really far when I felt excited.

But I hadn't realised the extent to which running solved everything. It bought me space to think, it earned me time to be alone without anyone needing anything from me, and it set me up for a day in which I felt better about myself.

My running was the same as another woman's scales: if I had a good run, I felt good about myself. Without my running, I felt bad and my mood was even worse. I was a hideous person, and saw no end in sight.

Worse still, the weight wasn't really going on.

Three weeks at 6,000 calories a day and no running, and I had put on less than half a stone. Miserable, puffy and being nagged by my husband to eat ALL THE BLOODY TIME, I was now officially nasty.

And this bloody stupid idea of a fat story to prove fat people were lazy had barely even begun. I was a class A twat with a first-class degree in being an arsehole, and my family was taking the full force of it.

Fat fact: when you feel bad about yourself, you make other people's lives a misery, then have that to feel guilty about too. This is a truth whether it is about exercise or about food.

Another truth is that misery and guilt become a massive part of the day. Imagine how much better we could be and how much more we could do if we felt less bad about ourselves. Or used up less of the space in our head arguing with the voice telling us we are bad, or ugly, or not good enough, or too fat.

Fat fact: feeling fat uses up headspace we know we could use doing better things.

The TV people were part of this journey of mine as well. One commissioner had put her own name against this project and had the balls to back me and risk that I wouldn't deliver, when thousands of others would not.

There was money invested in this project, and people's jobs, plus managers wanting results and deliverables to be met.

Alongside my own changing relationships with food, exercise, my family and my body, I had a job to get done. This project was a job: I had colleagues to work with in the film crew and the production company, and new bosses to answer to at the channel.

None of this was easy. Everything felt personal, was personal. This was my project and I wanted it done properly. The thought of doing anything inauthentic was unacceptable to me. I found the truth of this thing gripping – that so many lives can detonate emotionally because of our relationship with food and ourselves.

There were arguments. Big arguments.

Someone in the production company wanted stunts for the camera. They wanted me to eat until I was sick, and to capture it on film.

I hated the idea of stunts. I was angry at eating all the time, and livid that eating until I was sick was seen as good value for TV.

I get it, I really do. But I also remember telling everyone to fuck off, and if this was a fat story I didn't want to make it.

At moments like that, if I hadn't had a contract and a husband to hang on for, I would have quit.

I was summoned to the head of channel. I was not putting on weight fast enough and the bosses were concerned that I was not investing enough effort in getting as fat as I could. I was not delivering on my promise.

This was a major low in my life. I can still feel it now. It still makes me uncomfortable.

I was a stone or so heavier, looked hideous, felt rubbish. None of my clothes fit any more and I looked like a tub. I was eating all the time, going to bed full and waking up to face another day of food. I was not allowed to exercise and felt like I was going mad. It was made worse by the guilt I felt at being such an intolerable cow all the time at home. And now my boss was telling me I wasn't doing a good job.

Even my harshest critics will say I work damn hard and I always deliver. Without exception. This was the first time in my life that, when it came to effort, my bosses were unimpressed.

Fat fact: when you feel rubbish about yourself, criticism cuts even deeper and you seek comfort in something you can rely on to make you feel better.

Food loves you no matter what. It doesn't answer back, doesn't shout at you for being a cow, and cheers you up when your boss has made you feel miserable. If your boss tells you that you are rubbish, you may as well eat rubbish as well.

This was another lesson: when everything else goes wrong,

food can make you feel better. Except in my case, it made me feel worse.

The bosses took action. My food load went up to 8,000 calories a day, I was attached to a fitness tracker that counted my steps, and a feeder was dispatched for a week to force me to eat.

Despite quitting running, I was still walking around 10,000 steps a day: four school runs, a whip around my house and a dash to the train station soon add up.

Walking had to stop.

My kids loved it. We started taking a taxi to school and I took a taxi to the station. I have never felt so guilty in my life. I am a school-walk Nazi. I think it teaches kids to make an effort and to forget the car. The idea people would now see me shoving them in a taxi was mortifying.

The feeder turned up at my house. He was an ex-Marine, an athlete and a boot-camp instructor. My favourite sort of bloke: disciplined, enthusiastic and with my kind of humour. The kind that sees someone with a broken leg and tells them their good leg is looking mighty fine. Or sees someone crushed under a bus and bends down to tell them it could be worse, it could have been late.

He transposed the discipline of circuit training into food training. The four corners of my kitchen table were piled with high-fat foods; I had to down each pile in turn.

Peanut butter. Mars® Milk. More Mars® Milk. (Mars® Milk is one of the most highly calorific, high-fat things you can put into your body.) High-fat spread.

My new food diary looked like this:

0800: two litres Mars® Milk

0900: fully leaded cola

1000: a 500-calorie ready-meal (lasagne)

1100: fully leaded cola plus a chocolate bar

1200: two litres of Mars® Milk

Try not to be sick

1300: a ready-meal (fish and chips/cheese and chips) plus fully leaded cola

1400: one litre Mars® Milk

Rest

1500: one litre Mars® Milk

1600: half a jar of peanut butter

Try hard not to be sick

1800: full meal with family plus fully leaded cola

1900: chocolate pudding plus a tub of clotted cream

Rest

2100: one more ready-meal, more full-fat milk, ice cream

2300: one litre Mars® Milk.

Try this for a day and you will survive. You might even quite enjoy it. Try this for two days and you will want to quit. Try it for four days and you'll start to dread waking up because waking up means another day of food.

You dread the sound of the microwave going ping, signalling the start of another lasagne. Or the sickly smell of Mars® Milk, which still makes me gag when I so much as pass it in the supermarket aisle.

I was now a full-time eater and had practically given up on trying to be human. We went on a family holiday to

St Ives and I stood on our little balcony and cried and cried and cried, because I wasn't allowed to walk and was a miserable cow and now a crap mum, too.

All the things I would normally do with my children were forbidden. No walking around the town, no surfing on the beach, no bumbling about.

All the time I would usually have spent hip to hip with my family to make up for all the time I was on the road was being lost to a stupid project and a stupid film schedule which had been my own bloody stupid idea. I hated my fat story, hated my husband for saying it was a good idea, hated myself for doing it and even hated fat people for making me do it.

I blamed everyone and I made excuses for everything.

I was every fat person I ever criticise. I had suggested the bloody stupid idea, I had created the problem of fat me, and now I was blaming everyone else for it.

I was a miserable old bag to be around.

I finally realised what my running was really all about. I was an epileptic, which I considered a weakness; the health authorities had even given me a disabled badge. Running was my way of fighting back.

It made me feel fitter, tougher, better than the epilepsy that threatened to beat me. Better still if I could run in the rain or the snow or the ice. That just made it harder, tougher, to prove how tough I am on the inside.

I would run the morning after dislocating my shoulders the night before. I would run when my tongue was so badly bitten my mum couldn't understand me on the phone.

I wonder now if a lot of me was running away from things,

too. Running away from facing up to the fact that my epilepsy was catching up with me fast. And one day it might win...

I would do stupid stuff to impress myself. See someone ahead of me on the road and be determined to overtake them, even if I had to die in a sweaty puddle around the corner to recover.

I would hold my breath running fast by slower runners, to make it look like I wasn't even making an effort. I would do long jumps over grass verges to make it tougher. Essentially anything that would prove I was faster or fitter. When, in reality, I was a bit of a wreck.

Smoke and mirrors turned on myself.

So, fat me, unable to exercise, banned from walking, and shovelling 8,000 calories a day down my face, was suddenly exposed to reality: my epilepsy was way bigger than me. I had no running to hide behind or escape with. I was physically bankrupted by the whole thing, and it made me miserable.

I can honestly say I have never cried so much or so hard as the three months of being fat for *My Fat Story*. Not just because of the weight and being permanently uncomfortable, but because the thing that helped me keep my head above the water was gone too. For the first time in my life I felt ill-equipped to deal with anything – life, work or relationships.

I saw for the first time how much I depended on my 'uniform' to power through. In my dresses, I looked like the me I knew. In the baggy nonsense I now had to wear, I felt weaker, less powerful, less able to start on the front foot.

Going into a room, I was acutely aware I no longer looked

fit or skinny or like a runner. I looked like a chubby mum who doesn't care. I looked softer and felt weaker and hated every single moment of it.

I had originally thought some of the four stone would end up on my boobs, and for once in my life I would have boobs I could jiggle about and put in underwear.

Not a bit of it. Three of the four stone went between the tops of my thighs and the top of my ribs. I gained a gut of epic proportions. It was the sort of gut men get after drinking twenty pints a day for twenty years. A beer-gut-sized thing between my boobs and my front bum.

Or, if you think of it another way, a healthy eight-month baby.

In the queue for the bathroom in Marks and Spencer's, old ladies would smile at me kindly and let me go to the front of the line, thinking I was pregnant. I didn't have the heart to tell them it was just fat. Fat I gained on purpose to prove a sodding point.

I was sent flowers for the baby from a work colleague who had seen me and knew I would never be fat so must be preggers. And I was given seats on the Underground.

I felt shamed by not being honest about my project. I would accept the seats and sit down feeling horrible about myself and about not being truthful.

In fact, I was desperate to tell everyone what I was doing. I was desperate to let the kids tell other children, so other parents would know I wasn't really fat, just pretending. I was desperate to tell the people I saw every day what I was up to.

Fat photos appeared in the press and I was horrified. I knew I was doing a fat story, but seeing yourself looking fat is a really strange thing. And photos are one of the ways it hits home hardest.

The day my sheer size really hit me was when I walked past the window of a shop near where I live. I glanced in and saw this really big person – with my head on it. And then I realised it was wearing the same clothes as me. And, in fact, it was me.

I can still remember that feeling right now.

Other women have spoken to me about this same experience. There is something about the reflected image of ourselves that speaks to us very differently than the mirror at home.

Women have told me about the time they looked in a window and didn't recognise themselves. Or when they looked at a photo from a wedding or christening, saw themselves and finally decided it was enough, things had to change, they were not prepared to be that big woman any more.

It isn't just vanity. Vanity is a trivial thing, a superficial emotion. It's about being authentic to yourself. Fat women like I was, catching our reflection in the shop window, reject that person because it is not who we are. It is not the person we know.

The person we know is funny, or kind, or has a lovely family, or is tough, or used to be a runner for the army or be really good at tennis.

That woman in the reflection is just a fat woman. An invisible person who looks nothing like all the tough stuff you know yourself to be.

For me, this experience was temporary. For many, this is the truth of their lives. Avoiding their own reflection or photos of themselves, finding the images too upsetting to look at. Seeing the fat first, before seeing themselves or anything else.

I felt this too. I felt that now people saw me as fat before they even heard anything I said. I hated losing my voice this way, being disregarded because I was fatter than before.

I am ashamed of my vanity, too. Ashamed that I was desperate to tell everyone I was doing it for a programme. Desperate for the truth to come out so people would understand it wasn't the real me who was a fat person, just a temporary me.

I wanted an excuse.

And again, in this I was exactly the same as every fat person I have ever criticised. I wanted an excuse for being fat, something I could talk about to prove it was not my fault.

Excuses make you feel a whole lot better. I had one, and I desperately wanted to share it.

Month three and I was getting closer to my target weight of twelve stone, from my start point of just under eight and a half stone.

It was still a slog. The food was endless, the rows with my husband were fractious and he could not understand why I was finding this project so difficult when it is standard for me to commit to something and deliver on it without too much complaint.

This distance between us was hard. I felt he didn't understand. He felt I wasn't making enough effort to eat. And I felt horrible about myself. I dreaded the next mealtime and loathed my fat self.

I learned many practical things about being fat, too.

I learned why leggings and flip flops are so popular when you are fat. Especially when you have a gut like mine, which effectively means you have lost sight of your feet. Looking down, I hadn't seen my own bits for the best part of two months; I had to look in a mirror to see my own foof.

My mates christened my gut the gunt. Which works on the same basis as the cankle. Think about it. It is not pleasant.

My gunt was really quite something. It presented me with the same problem experienced by many fat people when it comes to dressing. Bits of me were a sturdy size 12 – a Marks and Spencer size 12, which is essentially a regular size 18. And other bits of me, like the circumference of my gunt, were a man-size XL.

My upper thighs were merging ever closer to becoming one solid trunk on which to balance the giant ball of my body.

And so on came the leggings.

Leggings are the death of hope. Once you buy and wear leggings, you are accepting comfort and ease over the hope of ever getting a grip on your life and size.

It doesn't matter if you buy them in a zebra print, a leopard skin or that special extra-cheap variety that shows some skin too, and your pants if you are wearing any. They are still stretchy pants for people who have accepted that the cheeseburgers have won.

Leggings pretend to be a size 10 or 12 or whatever lie makes you feel better, and expand ever outwards so you never have to concern yourself that they may be getting a bit tight and therefore you may be shoving a bit too much food in your face.

Adding a pair of slide-on shoes means you never even have to contemplate the fact that your gut is now so big that trying to reach over it to do up your shoes is painful. When it became painful for me to reach down to tie up the laces on my trainers (now the only shoes I was able to fit my fat feet into), I bought slides too.

So there I was, three stone heavier, in leggings and slide-on shoes, looking like every fat person about whom I have ever wondered what the hell they were doing with their lives and why they had given up.

It is easy to do. It is the easiest thing in the world, in fact. To keep rearranging the way you manage your life and work around your big old body so you never have to front up to it, never have to deal with it.

When you no longer fit proper clothes, you buy clothes that expand to fit. When your gut makes it painful to bend over, you buy slides. When you are so fat everything is sweaty and uncomfortable, feeling comfy is everything.

I know women who dread shopping. They refuse to go into a clothes shop to try something on. Or will only try stuff on if there are proper doors that lock. They dread the mirrors and the huge windows of passers-by looking into the shop.

Chubby me walked by the windows of Reiss, where I used to shop, and was struck by the memory of how the skinny me used to fly in, grab a dress, throw it on, buy it and be out – all in a heartbeat.

Chubby me wouldn't even go through the door. Floor-length mirrors in the middle of the store. Floor-length windows with everyone looking in. Not to mention the shop assistants, who are all a size 8 and look pretty darn good in all the merchandise. Imagine them seeing my gunt!

I understand how off-putting it all is. And how avoiding the issue altogether, and buying stretchy things that will fit no matter how big you are, is the way to deal with this problem.

By now I was pushing twelve stone, having gained nearly half my original bodyweight. I wasn't allowed to walk, was struggling with basic jobs like getting dressed, and was about as miserable as I imagine it is possible to be.

Some will say that twelve stone is nothing. That they long to be twelve stone. That twelve stone is aspirational.

I have heard these comments and they are fair.

But it is a relative thing. Imagine taking nearly half your weight, then adding it on. If you are sixteen stone now, imagine gaining eight stone. That's where I was. That's what I had done. Added another half me on top of me.

Even the Harley Street doctors monitoring my fat journey to keep a fair account of my progress were alarmed.

I was now registering as obese on their BMI chart and my liver was starting to shout. A fatty liver is a side effect of shoving on weight faster than your body can handle it. I was sent off for tests to check my organs would withstand the experiment.

Facing up to medical staff was always a strange conversation. Trying to get them to understand I was doing this on purpose took for ever, and trying to get them to accept this was also my idea took even longer.

It is unfathomable to health professionals that anyone would do this to their own body to prove a point.

In many ways, I was with them. It was unfathomable to me that I had let myself get into this state to prove a point. Without the personal pressure I felt from having committed to my bosses and the people investing in the programme, I would have given up, and I would have failed.

I was every woman who committed to a journey with their weight but, feeling miserable and fed up about their world, would have given in.

I was no better than them.

And I think this was at the heart of all that matters about *My Fat Story*.

It started as an experiment to prove fat people are lazy and this whole weight problem is easy to solve.

But as I grew fatter, the layers of our relationship with everything – from how we dress, to how we get on with our husbands, to the real fear of the high street, to the way the scales dictate our day – became clear.

I quickly became every fat person I criticise. I wanted an excuse to explain this all away, I wanted to give up, I wanted to crawl into a little corner and not leave my house, because that was easier than facing the world as a person I didn't even recognise in a reflection in a shop window.

I lost my confidence and I lost me. I remember accepting an invitation to go on *Celebrity Juice* as fat me. I dreaded it, because so much of my being bold relied on me feeling tougher than, fitter than, stronger than. If nothing else, I always looked like I could probably run faster than my critics.

I knew what I would wear, I knew how I would look, and I

could pretend to be tough and let the criticisms and the gags at my expense wash over me like the rest of the stuff I face on Twitter on a daily basis.

Now a blancmange of a woman, I had lost that uniform of self-protection. I had lost me under a layer of fat and all the issues that come with it. I had taken myself, my family and my self-confidence to a very dark place indeed.

I was fat. I hated it. And I hated myself.

It was time for me to have my fat photoshoot.

It wasn't pretty. The gunt was really something. So much so that the media rejected the images as being faked. Most thought I was wearing a fat suit. Or had some kind of prosthesis attached to my gut.

I knew I had succeeded. If the media thought it was too unreal to be true, it was a sure measure that what I had done would be shocking enough to capture the imagination of those who were feeling just the same as me.

A woman I didn't recognise. A stranger I didn't want the world to see.

My Fat Story remains the most successful commission for TLC since its launch, and sold worldwide and was highly commended in the Best Popular Factual Broadcast, Digital Award at the Digital Broadcast Awards 2015.

More importantly, *My Fat Story* got a legion of men and women up off their sofa, moving more and eating less. And Fat Club is still going strong, offering free help, support and encouragement to anyone wanting to start their own journey to feeling better about their lives.

You can find out more about the rules of Fat Club and how to join via the Facebook group run by Amy and Lydia, founding members of 'Fat Club – Eat Less & Move More'. Or via Twitter @FatClub10000.

CHAPTER 12

LAST WORDS

And so, my friend, this is where our cosy chat ends. And, funnily enough, I don't want it to be over.

I had dreaded writing this book, because I have the tenacity of a dead rabbit and am about as far from a completer-finisher as Stephen Hawking is from finishing a London Marathon.

But actually, I have loved it. Loved spending time with my own thoughts. And sneaking away to write about bits of my life long filed on my shelf in a box marked 'past'.

It's felt a little bit like taking your phone into the toilet with you when you go for a wee: five minutes of time to yourself, facing inwards, away from all the things in your life that pull you outward in a thousand different directions – your kids who need you to do something, your husband who needs you to find something, your boss who needs you to do his bidding, your mother who needs you to hear that she is cross at the neighbour, your friend who needs somewhere to park.

It's been very much like therapy. Awkward at times, like being made to sit in front of a mirror and just stare at yourself and say what you see (my idea of a nightmare). But therapeutic just the same.

I wonder how it is for someone reading all this. I feel embarrassed at the thought – kind of like waking up the morning after the night before and vaguely remembering an incident with a policeman and a kipper and telling the kebab man he has a small willy. I prefer not to think about actual people reading this book (if any bugger actually does). I am choosing to imagine this is our little secret, just you and me tucked up in the darkest corner of a pub behind a sticky table.

I wonder if you are thinking, 'Thank God that's bloody well over,' as you see the end in sight and look forward to heading out the door of the pub, happy to be rid of that bloody, whining old cow-bag as you hot-foot it onto the night-bus home.

I wonder if, for you, this whole chat has been like one of those dreadful nights when you agree to have a drink with someone you were never too sure about in the first place, only to spend the next torturous three hours remembering why you were never too sure about them. Because they are a desperate, needy, narcissistic, deluded, paranoid, lonely bore and are about as good company as low-level chlamydia, perhaps?

Maybe the experience of spending time with me has been like one of those nights where you meet someone you've secretly always found pretty funny or agreed with occasionally and thought it would be a good laugh to have a few wines with, and it turns out we have ended up sharing two bottles of Prosecco and four G&Ts and are now committed to being bestest friends for ever and loving each other even though we only get to see each other once a year.

I sort of hope it's the latter. But I am honestly content if it's not.

You can't write about yourself and demand people like the person they see; that seems disingenuous from the outset.

You can only speak your truth and share it. If you are prepared to put it out there, you have to be prepared for people to tell you it is a bag of crap. (See Amazon feedback written by my secret antifa fan club for details.)

As with so many things in life, you do have a choice: if you don't like being beaten up you can sit at home on your sofa and shut up instead.

I certainly feel like it's been therapy for my soul. (Which is a bit of a red flag right there. Therapy is the preserve of my epic Jewish mates and Americans, and I am neither. Even the word 'therapy' suggests a situation in which you are trapped and bored shitless, and wondering how to get the hell out before you fall into a deep vegetative state from which you might never recover.)

I have over-shared and the ramifications are that this over-sharing will now be pulled about and regurgitated here and there in the press to prove whatever grand malevolence I am supposed to be guilty of this week.

I accept this as my punishment. I also accept that I do not control the edit – others do, you do. My detractors will extract whichever bits of the book they believe confirm the things they already think about me. And they may even have a point.

Because all the things in this book – these words, this blah blah blah – are my truths. This is the stuff of my life, the mistakes, the warts (genital and otherwise), the disasters and the triumphs; the lot.

I hope that by reading it some people will have found something helpful for their own lives, or perhaps found we have some things in common, even the things we wildly disagree about (which, for many, is about 90 per cent of what comes out of my mouth).

I hope it will give some of you the courage to believe you are right to have your own views, whatever they are. And that you are brave and beautiful, and what other people say really doesn't matter if you find the strength not to let it. Sometimes we all need help finding that strength and reminding ourselves that real life happens offline. Try to make like an arrow and feel the criticism whoosh past you as you fly ahead.

It's OK to read negative stuff about yourself. Being able to watch people write about how your nose is big or you look like a lesbian, and challenge yourself to read such things dispassionately, is a good skill. You have to find the strength to step outside and smell the air and realise that all those people walking down the road don't give a monkey's about what the hell is being said on Twitter or posted on Instagram – about you or anyone else.

It's all noise. And you have the volume control.

You know how if you ask ten people for feedback and only one person says something bad, that bad review shouts much louder than the nine really good ones? Life is exactly like that. Get others to help you listen to the nine voices; train yourself to hear them. Listen to the nine. Challenge yourself to do something useful with the tenth: process it; recognise that someone is probably looking to detract from your strengths; put it in the box marked 'their issues'.

Other people need to own their issues. You don't. Don't carry them around or let them drag you down.

I hope that some of the people kind enough to buy this thing have found it just a bit interesting, like looking into someone else's shopping trolley to see what size Tampax they take, or peeking into someone's kitchen window as you walk past. I hope that by looking into bits of my life and some of the stuff that has happened in it, they will see that it's OK for us not to take ourselves or our jobs too seriously, and it is absolutely OK to laugh at ourselves a bit more than we do.

It's OK for people somewhat in the public eye to admit they are a bit hopeless sometimes, or have done some pretty awful things.

To say they stole someone's husband, or thought about taking a hitman out on their first. To admit that not all babies are actually that cute and some kids are downright feral (usually the ones called Destiny or Belle).

Or that they were secretly OK when their grandad died because the last six months were so awful for their mum that they raged at the cruelty of medicine; or they wouldn't want a disabled child because they just aren't that good a mum; or openly mock a man for having a micro penis. Maybe all that is actually just being honest, and not such a bad thing as long as they aren't forcing their beliefs on anyone else.

If my life were a house, I'd make a really crap estate agent. I've shown you round without buying fresh flowers to make the kitchen look nice, or baking fresh bread or turning on all the lights so you think it looks homely.

I've shown you the ugly, unattractive bits people normally hide. The smelly damp bits in the corner. The ongoing row with the neighbours about my bush (or hedge, if you prefer).

I've shown you my dating disasters, my career nightmares and the multiple times my big gob has got me into a whole world of pain.

I've told you about being in trouble with the police and the court system, and how I even had social services call about the welfare of my kids, thanks to my detractors.

And how I've waged war against the left, the system, the establishment, anyone to do with HR or compliance, the state broadcaster, and those too certain of their own importance.

I've even told you about my epilepsy – the biggest battle of the lot.

And, you know, I feel pretty good about it all. And about myself. I am just this, nothing more, bad bits and all, and I am not too proud to show it, or to pretend to hide it.

I am my most powerful me: unashamed, unafraid and a little unhinged by the madness of my life.

And I am certain about what matters. I am proud of my children and my husband. And of all the people in my country who love it and want the best for it, and the bits of my country that are great.

This brilliant country is filled with people I love being around. Who have different views to mine, or the same, who are happy to talk about them, to disagree over a pint and to end as friends.

Who can find the fun in the simple things in life, and take the piss when they are hurting the most.

People who would always stop to help you if you needed them. Or come and defend your honour if it needed it. Or leave a car-park ticket in the meter if there is still an hour left on it.

People who tell you when you did something well, and call you out for being an arsehole just the same. Or warn you that you're being a right twat and need to wind your neck in, or that, in fact, the new hairstyle that you thought was really snazzy in the salon actually looks like a bag of crap on you.

These are the people I like to be with and belong to. These are my kind of Brits. It is not all pretty and polite. We all have a crap boiler or a sister that pisses us off or a kid that is too spoiled or a dog that is too fat.

We all have stuff we hide, to pretend to the world we have got our lives in order or even to pretend to ourselves so the day goes along OK.

We don't all feel strong all the time. Sometimes we have to pretend while the rest of us catches up. I have spent many days doing just that.

These are the weaknesses that allow us to get along with each other, even as we pretend we have got our shit together so that someone will employ us, or love us, or give us a mortgage, or lend us money. It is the weaknesses we share that make us stronger together.

Which is why London and the liberals have got it so wrong. They have created an environment in which another, devastating kind of pretending has become law – in which not only must we never say certain things out loud, we must pretend we don't even think them. They tell us which thoughts are permissible and can be spoken, and which we must hide.

It is now racist to observe how Asians love to stand in the doorway of the Tube while they work out where they are going, oblivious to the forty people behind them who just want to get to work. It's Islamophobic to say that Muslims really aren't that creative when it comes to naming their children, despite the fact that if I stand in a playground in Leicester and shout Mohammed, 4,562 children will come running.

It is now sexist to say women and men are not equal and should not all be paid the same. That no two people are equal; that no two people put the same effort into the same job or achieve the same outcome, and that gender usually isn't the differentiator.

It is officially fattist to say that it's not healthy to shove half the fridge in your face, become morbidly obese and then think it's OK to ask the taxpayer to pay for the new hip you now need, or for your type 2 diabetes treatment.

It's misogynistic to say anything other than that women are awesome and their vaginas are made of steel. As if that were enough.

It's fascist to say that Trump was democratically elected as the 45th President. Or that Brexiteers won with 52 per cent of the vote.

It's racist to say that Caster Semenya should not be allowed to compete in the female 800-metre race because she has internal testes and hormone levels three times that of a normal female.

It's homophobic to say that, much as I love Gay Pride, I cannot abide the way that even in these tolerant processionals certain individuals are excluded – viz the 2017 march at which the Israeli Pride flag in a rainbow was deemed offensive and those marching with it were asked to remove themselves from the event.

It's transphobic to say I agree entirely with Donald Trump that trans individuals should not serve in the military. I am delighted you are trans – I could not be happier for you. But the idea that this is something we need in our military, when there are other individuals who will not need the same level of cost to recruit and retain, then, for me, the simple economic argument wins every time.

The Crown Prosecution Service has just issued new guidance as to what constitutes hate. Now it's enough that you perceive someone to deserve the label, even if you have no proof.

The Association of Chief Police Officers and the CPS have agreed a common definition of hate crime:

> Any criminal offence which is perceived by the victim or any other person, to be motivated by hostility or prejudice based on a person's race or perceived race; religion or perceived religion; sexual orientation or perceived sexual orientation; disability or perceived disability and any crime motivated by hostility or prejudice against a person who is transgender or perceived to be transgender.

What madness it this? Perceptions and hurty feelings. Smoke and mirrors.

And guidance like this makes things worse, not better. The more we break down into different identity groups, the more labels there are.

I've been called them all. They are a lazy thing, flung out carelessly in the hope that at least one will stick, activating any group with sufficient power to lobby to have you fired or arrested.

So if you identify as black, you've got 'racist' in your armoury, to fling at anyone who crosses you. If you identify as a Muslim, you've got 'racist' and 'Islamophobe'. If you are a black Muslim lesbian, you have 'racist', 'Islamophobe' and 'homophobe'.

The one with the most identities gets the most weapons in their personal arsenal. It's like a weird game of Top Trumps for victims.

And when people start to conflate their politics with their identity, then things get really personal.

If, for example, you are a Remainer, and I criticise Remain, I am perceived to be criticising you personally.

That is exactly what we saw over Brexit. Legions of close friends and kitchen-supper mates fell out over Brexit. If one voted Remain and one voted Brexit, they could no longer be friends. Not even on Facebook. And this was not teenage kids – this went on among fully grown adults, unable to remain friends with people they had loved for years because their identity and their politics were confused as being one and the same.

Even the Johnson family fell out. Boris was Brexit. His sister Rachel sat on the beach in Cannes on 24 June and wept because she was Remain; later she became a temporary Liberal Democrat in protest (some things get taken too far).

If I try to silence your opinion, I am no longer simply criticising your politics. Identity politics means I am now criticising you personally. If I speak out with my belief that Black Lives Matter is a nonsense organisation that needs to stop what it's doing because it fuels civil unrest – an opinion supported by the niece of Martin Luther King, whom I met in a hotel lobby – then I am not criticising your politics, I am criticising you as a black woman, giving you the legitimacy to label me a racist.

Despite the fact that I am not, that we might agree on lots of other issues, and that we might have been friends.

In this climate, any attack on the things you believe is an attack on your very humanity, which explains why men are so isolated from the feminist debate; appearing to attack womankind is dangerous. I, on the other hand, can say what I like about women; I might be called a misogynist (I frequently am), but I won't be prosecuted for it, because I am a woman.

That's why I carefully referenced Martin Luther King's niece above. I need the voice of a black woman to say that Black Lives Matter needs to stop because if I say it, as a white woman, I will be labelled a racist. Plus, it's hard to argue with someone called Luther King.

That's also why I invited the beautiful Mohan Singh onto my radio show to talk about Muslim grooming gangs. Mohan is a Sikh. I've already referenced my undying love for Sikhs.

If I talk about grooming gangs, I can only reach the people who probably already agree with my views or are prepared to listen to my views and occasionally agree. I cannot reach the people who reject my views and anything I do or say outright simply because it is me. Perhaps because they can't see past the labels – Islamophobe, racist, Brexiteer, xenophobe, whatever. I accept that.

But if Mohan Singh talks about grooming gangs, whatever his views, we start to reach the people who won't listen to me but might listen to him, even if they disagree. That's the beauty of having multiple voices. And it's something our media should be doing a great deal more of: using lots of different voices to reach more people, to get messages out there, to draw people into conversation, even if it's to disagree. Too often these days, programmes are made with compelling contributors to force a point of consensus or to air a specific viewpoint approved by the programme editor.

The result is that whole swathes of England go unspoken for. Hundreds of thousands without a voice. Largely because of those who play identity politics and throw labels about.

Hillary Clinton's campaign was based entirely on this same identity politics and the idea of intersectionality – the ways in which oppressive institutions (racist, sexist, homophobic, transphobic, ableist, xenophobic, classist, etc.) are interconnected and cannot be examined separately from one another.

Hillary Clinton campaigned at the apex of intersectionality. She campaigned for every different group on the basis that the thing that mattered most to them was their identity.

She campaigned for women, for Hispanics, for gays, for black women, for black lesbian women and for the disabled.

Basically, if you saw yourself as a minority or, in my terms, a victim, then you were invited to vote for Hillary.

And of course it turned out not to be enough. Identity politics is never enough. It speaks only to how you see yourself. It does not speak to how you see the future direction of the country.

What Hillary Clinton had in terms of politically correct soundbites about gender or race, she lacked in actual policies or concrete things she was committed to making happen. That's why she lost.

Even her running mate was selected because of his Hispanic credentials. The crowd went wild on the campaign when he spoke to them in Spanish. As if speaking Spanish were, by itself, enough.

Clinton may have gained some support through her identity politics, but she lost because of identity politics too; ultimately it was limiting.

And I think that's reassuring. At a time when everyone is competing to be the biggest victim, the argument for action and clear policy is still greater and can be heard more clearly.

I see it today. And it leads me on to my own future and what's next.

What's next for Katie Hopkins?

I have to say, there has never been a master plan. I have never been that calculating or that clear about where I was headed. I just followed my gut, wrote stuff, and sometimes got paid to keep writing the stuff I wanted to write.

But things are changing. And have changed.

I see how the media has shifted into a deeply paranoid space where the cost of doing business, in every sense, is much greater than before.

There is real money and power sitting with campaign and lobbying groups who have strong links to politics and power, and the support of identity groups. Take the Muslim Council of Britain, for example. Or the Board of Deputies of British Jews. Add Hope Not Hate, which is very well funded, and you have the triumvirate of lobbying power. These guys can pull in the chief rabbi or the head imam to make their point, and they lobby editors incessantly to get their views heard most loudly across Britain.

They work tactically. They pick out sponsors, haul them out in the press, encourage their supporters to target the sponsors, and work as a mob – a mob defined by identity, sent forth by the heads of the identity they are loyal to, to try to sever commercial ties between advertisers and the media platform they espouse.

Then you have the power players like Clooney, Murdoch Junior and Gates, who donate millions to those who seek to censor opinions from the right or from supporters of Trump.

Place all that in a climate of paranoia and fear and it quickly becomes apparent that this is not a good time to be a journalist fighting from the right. It's a time in which labels are incendiary and entire legions of lawyers and litigators exist to pounce on the smallest perceived misdemeanours. Not to mention the appetite of the CPS and police for a Conservative scalp.

The Sun ran an article about the Muslim grooming gangs, referring to The Muslim Problem in capital letters; it lost an MP her position on the front bench, even though she had nothing to do with the article that caused the perceived offence. It nearly cost Trevor Kavanagh his job on *The Sun*. And he has worked there for twenty years.

Before that, it was Kelvin MacKenzie. Admittedly I thought he was a prize pillock, and so did most of the News UK building by all accounts, but that is neither here nor there. Through no direct fault of his own, he ended up 'agreeing to leave' over a column – because the aforementioned powerful lobbying groups managed to force him out.

I can't even tell you some of the things the Mail Online has had to pay to 'correct' or 'compensate for' on my behalf, but you would fall off your chair. It's enough to make you spit. And lawyers have no qualms about which ambulance they have to chase – even if it involves compensation for a terrorist set out to harm our people or our way of life.

It is moments like this that make me want to give it all up. It is a dirty business. Moments like being criticised by Ofcom for being too pro-Israeli on my radio show, but then fired from the same radio show for tweeting something perceived as anti-Jewish, despite the fact that I was referencing an Islamist attack.

Or being hounded for saying something on Twitter that someone deemed offensive. Or having a selfie taken in a Sicilian street with some random bloke who happened to be linked to Holocaust denial. (What do people expect – that I ask for a CV from everyone I have a selfie with?)

There is no rationalising with these people.

I see that the world is changing. I see that the ability to speak out is being lost. That the platform from which to speak has shrunk down to its smallest size yet. And the direction of travel is still toward an ever-increasingly identity-bound form of politics.

It is a great pity and a great shame.

Sometimes I feel like a polar bear on a little island of ice where a whole polar ice-cap used to be, watching the land under my feet melt away. The old industry has changed; the media is controlled by those who think like Clinton, and socialism rules.

It will not be like this for ever. Politics and market forces come in phases, and this is a phase. But it is a phase I will not enjoy very much in my present form or position. I don't want to keep trying to speak out while the doors and windows are repeatedly slammed against me; eventually my tongue will get caught.

We need new ways, new platforms, new opportunities to speak out more freely and to keep standing up for the people in this country who feel like they have lost their voice.

And I am committed to doing that. Because it is what I know, and because I believe in doing it. Also because there are too many people out there who feel utterly dejected at the state of the country and a capital city that increasingly looks and sounds like a foreign country. And I don't mean anything to do with colour or background; I mean foreign in its true sense, as in a place where the natives have become the outsiders. A place where our own customs, rituals, language or behaviours take second place. A place we no longer feel at home.

I feel responsible for standing up against all that. I would feel disloyal if I just shut up shop and left it all behind for the good life – even though that temptation is pulling me hard. There is a massive part of me that could quite happily stop all this, sit quietly in my garden and dig things about a bit, maybe get the rescue chickens I have wanted for ages, and a pig. That is where my heart is set. That's my plan for a little later in my life.

Right now, voices are needed more than ever before. This is

no time to quit. It is the time to find a way to keep speaking. To move to self-funded filming and documentary work that bypasses commissioners and TV consorts. To find a Twitter-like platform that bypasses the censor's mob. And to keep writing stuff that is honest and true and find a platform on which to post it.

This is not about the numbers. It never has been.

If no one listened to my radio show or read my column or even likes this book, I would understand. It's just me talking to people about my thoughts and my life.

But if people are interested and like it, then so much the better. The fact that my radio show was the fastest-growing, that my column was the most read, that this book is in your hands and you are reading these words right now – that is a lovely thing and it's the fuel that drives me to keep doing what I do.

Whether we agree or not, whether you like me or not, whether we think completely differently but still shared a laugh – I want to thank you for stopping a while with me to chat.

Now go, you good thing. Go into the world. Be the person you are on the inside, and say what the bloody hell you like and don't let anyone make you feel small.

You are big and beautiful and brave. No one knows your legs aren't shaved or your husband shoved half a cucumber up your jacksy last night just for the giggles. (This has not happened to me – just to be clear.)

Opinions are not right or wrong. And no one is better than you. Or has more right to a view.

You stand strong and come home happy. Or if you need a cry, cry until you are so ugly only your dog will show you love.

Do you. And do it well.

Go, you good thing, go. xx